DRIVING
CHANGE

DRIVING
CHANGE

The UPS Approach to Business

MIKE BREWSTER
AND
FREDERICK DALZELL

NEW YORK

Library of Congress Cataloging-in-Publication Data has been applied for.

ISBN-10: 1-4013-0288-2
ISBN-13: 978-1-4013-0288-7

Hyperion books are available for special promotions,
premiums, or corporate training.
For details contact Michael Rentas, Proprietary Markets,
Hyperion, 77 West 66th Street, 12th floor, New York, New York 10023,
or call 212-456-0133.

Design by Jo Anne Metsch

FIRST EDITION

10   9   8   7   6   5   4   3   2   1

To past and current
UPS employees

CONTENTS

ACKNOWLEDGMENTS

THIS BOOK COULD NEVER have been written without the unwavering support and enthusiasm of UPS and the literally hundreds of employees who worked so hard to make sure we got the story right and experienced the many varied aspects of the company.

Several members of the company's management team carved time out of their schedules to sit for interviews. CEO Mike Eskew took part in two separate discussions. David Abney and Kurt Kuehn—COO and head of sales and marketing, respectively—not only were gracious in allowing numerous interviews but invariably returned emails and telephone calls quickly, as well. Other management team members that gave generously of their time include Dave Barnes, Bob Stoffel, and Christine Owens.

Former executives who were particularly helpful include former CEOs Jim Kelly and Oz Nelson, former COO John Beystehner, as well as Lea Soupata, Frank Erbrick, Joe Tranfo, Don Layden, and Charlie Adams.

Ken Sternad, director of public relations at UPS, first conceived of a book that would mark the company's 2007 centennial, and then insisted that it become a vehicle not for just lauding UPS but for exploring the role that the company plays in the global marketplace. Ken's advice and insights early on in the project not only formed the book's trajectory, but steered us toward the management lessons that were eventually included.

Steve Soltis and Bruce Danielson, members of Ken's executive communications team, were each indispensable in their own ways and executed a pitch-perfect passing of the baton. Steve offered critical structural and editorial advice early on, and Bruce carried the project over the goal line, performing close editing and working with the UPS management team to ensure successive drafts included their latest thoughts and comments.

Other UPS corporate public relations/communications team members who were particularly helpful include Mark Giuffre in Louisville and Norman Black and Lynnette McIntire in Atlanta. UPS archivist Jill Swiecichowski not only located important documents and materials, but also answered many email requests about UPS history. Several UPS drivers consented to have us ride with them, including Rudy Taylor in New York, Gary Duggan in Cambridge, Massachusetts, Ed Murphy in Norwood, Massachusetts,

Chen Wei Feng in Shanghai, Patrick De Keersmaecker in Brussels, and Senol Demircan in Istanbul.

Anyone familiar with UPS will appreciate how its devotion to efficiency and organization would be immensely helpful to the writer/reporter traveling overseas. Several UPS employees in Europe and Asia took entire days out of their lives to ensure that things went smoothly for us. Joe Guerrisi was our guide through Singapore and Hong Kong, while Daryl Tay spent several days helping us navigate both the highways and cuisine of Guangdong Province and Shanghai.

Ken Torok, head of UPS Asia, was a gracious and helpful host for that entire trip, and China country manager Richard Loi and his team patiently explained the all-important story of UPS in China. In Europe, Carsten Helssen was Mike's road trip partner throughout Belgium, Germany, and the Netherlands, setting up interviews and smoothing out the inevitable logistical snafus with grace and good humor. Hans-Peter Teufers also traveled in Germany and Poland with Mike and explained the many public affairs issues that affect UPS in Europe, and Shaun Grantham of the southern Europe UPS team handled those duties in Istanbul. In Louisville, Mike Mangeot guided Fred through the company's airline operations.

Unfortunately, we can't name every person from UPS who contributed to this book, due to the sheer volume of names. So, a genuine "thank you" goes out to everyone who either submitted to an interview, facilitated interviews, or provided requested information. Special thanks are extended to, in no particular order: Rocky Romanella, Vern Higberg, Larry Bloomenkranz, Cindy Miller, Jack Levis, Dr. Ranganath Nuggehalli, John Flick, Joe Perillo, Pat Moran, Dave De Leon, Mike deLong, Bill Hook, Mark Hale, Bill Driscoll, John Wheeler, Rino Bergonzi, Andy Connelly, Tom Murphy, Joerns Reineke, Uwe Detering, Engin Sarioglu, Koknar Tezay, Annette Storr, Wolfgang Flick, Wolfgang Nast, Haluk Undeger, Arzu Undeger, Wojciech Arszewski, Patrice Andre, Frank Sportolari, Mary Yao, Vichai Chuensuksawadi, Jeannie Tay, W.K. Wong, Jacek Przybylowski, Jim Medeiros, Ed Zolcinski, John Nallin, Leon Williams, Bram van de Burgt, Abby Nathisuwan, Ava Ho, Sebastian Chan, Phillip Critton, Steve Okun, Brian Cusson, Jennifer Wong, Billie Tan, Janice Chan, and Jenny Cao.

For other favors great and small performed by non-UPS employees, Mike would like to thank Dr. Jeff Sonnenfeld, Steve Fox, Geoff Garth, Wayne Guay, Harold Tanner, Dave Randle, Sandra Davis, Elisha Yanay, John Mazzella, Dr. Jeanne Ross, and Dr. Benn Konsynski. In the daytime gig Mike had for much of the writing of this book, Pat Wood and Michelle Lansing were incredibly generous in allowing him to take time off and travel for the book. Amey Stone's support, optimism, and understanding made a challenging and time-consuming project much more enjoyable.

Fred would like to thank Mary-Elise Connolly for her constant support, as well as Abigail and Molly Dalzell for their enthusiasm.

From historical consultancy the Winthrop Group, founding partner Dave Dyer was extremely helpful in shaping this project early on and providing perspective from his career of telling some of the biggest stories in Corporate America. Jenny Beveridge, Winthrop's business manager, was extremely helpful in responding to questions and helping with expenses, travel, and various writer-induced crises. Alex Fuller was a Winthrop intern in 2006 whose public record research was of great assistance.

Betsy Lerner of Dunow Carlson Lerner is the embodiment of today's literary agent, expected to execute deals, edit text, and serve as a sounding board for ideas. Betsy did all this and more. Hyperion's Zareen Jaffery and Will Schwalbe brought several excellent ideas to improve the book's readability, presentation, and marketing.

On the Road with UPS

RIDE WITH THE DRIVERS, you're told. If you really want to find out what makes the world's leading package delivery and logistics company tick, if there is anything valuable for today's managers to learn from UPS, it all starts with the drivers. Mention UPS to anyone, anywhere, and you'll hear immediately about *their* driver: Rudy or Murph or Patrick or Chen or Sue.

So on a sweltering July morning, you find yourself admiring a Snoopy made entirely of lilies at Preston Bailey, a celebrity flower arranger on West 25th Street in New York City. A COD package from UPS for $68.15 has set off a mild tempest at the business, with employees scurrying to deal with long-time UPS driver Rudy Taylor.

Rudy politely but firmly withholds the package from a young woman increasingly anxious to tear it out of his hands. Finally, the business manager lopes in. "When Rudy says you need to write a check, you write a check," he announces to the small staff, signs for the package, grabs a Krispy Kreme donut, and disappears.

Not fully out of Preston Bailey's, Rudy is explaining that the business manager's signature has by now been uploaded into the UPS worldwide tracking system, and that the sender can already see on UPS.com that the package has arrived at Preston Bailey. You start to think that maybe today's UPS has as much to do with technology as it does with drivers.

So you go to Mahwah, New Jersey, to UPS's World Technology Headquarters. Each day, data on some fifteen million packages wends its way through the UPS global network. At 8:15 A.M. sharp each weekday morning, about fifty managers responsible for maintaining the system gather in a large conference room to diagnose, detect, and fix any problems. Think of those Apple Store Genius Bars, where Apple aficionados bring their iPods and iMacs to be cured, but on a much grander scale.

Jim Medeiros, the UPS manager in charge, and his team discuss any potentially serious technology issue at any of UPS's 8,000 hubs, distribution centers, or package-sorting facilities around the world that might have developed during the previous twenty-four hours. It doesn't matter where in the world a UPS package is, Medeiros says, all package information is maintained on the global UPS system, enabling the company to act as one worldwide company. This is a claim worth checking.

So you go to Futian, a twenty-five-block free trade zone in the southern Chinese city of Shenzhen. Inside a 300,000-square-foot UPS distribution center, tens of thousands of McDonald's Happy Meal toys heading for South America are stacked more than twenty-six feet high. They sit next to W.W.W. Gore coats, Lexmark inkjet printers and Molex fiber optic cables. For these and other customers in Futian, UPS arranges ocean freight, air freight, and ground transportation, from the manufacturer to the warehouse to retail stores.

But it soon becomes apparent that technology, too, has its limits, and that UPS must get creative to serve its customers in every corner of the planet. In the southern African nation of Zambia, for example, UPS uses canoes to make deliveries across the Zambezi River. On the other end of Africa, mules deliver UPS packages into villages in the Abu Simbel region of Egypt. Near the famous cathedral in the narrow streets of Cologne, Germany, UPS cyclists deliver documents and packages to downtown offices. But what do all of these local services have to do with big-picture global trade routes, with those supply chains that we all hear so much about?

So you go to Chicago, to a UPS–sponsored conference on the global economy called Longitudes. Globally savvy CEOs debate the economic integration of Asia and the removal of trade barriers through organizations like the World Trade Organization (WTO). Former U.S. trade representative Charlene Barshefsky asserts that the United States needs to eliminate its budget deficit. Pulitzer Prize–winning author Daniel Yergin advises U.S. policy makers to concentrate on managing oil interdependence, as becoming energy independent is unrealistic. All important issues, certainly, but how is UPS itself connected to all of them?

So you go to UPS corporate headquarters in Atlanta. Mike Eskew, UPS's chairman and chief executive officer, sits in the company cafeteria and sips from his mug as he talks about postal codes in Germany, time studies in Bloomington, and overflow volumes in Pittsburgh.

He casts his industrial engineer's gaze around the room at colleagues striding by. Despite the Fortune 500 trappings of manicured grounds, a state-of-the-art employee gym, and gadget-laden conference rooms, there's something a little different about the culture at UPS's corporate headquarters.

UPS employees are not permitted to eat or drink at their desks, a nod of solidarity to those working in the field in hubs and package cars, which even the top brass observes. Company meetings start exactly on time, campus buses pull up at their assorted stops right on schedule, and clean-cut tour guides deliver rehearsed presentations flawlessly.

"You know, going all the way back to our founder, Jim Casey, we have had this extraordinary culture, this culture of constructive dissatisfaction," Eskew says. "Jim Casey is still a strong presence here, because the things he said are true even today." Now Eskew is talking about—ghosts?

No. You realize that he is saying that maybe UPS's century-long success is about something more than driving trucks and sorting packages and wiring mainframes and flying airplanes. Maybe it's also about the simple values that Casey embraced, about a singular culture of never being satisfied, about the discipline to execute, about the willingness of tens of thousands of like-minded people to pull together and transform an organization. Maybe it's about—surprise!—managing large-scale change.

So you don't go anywhere else. You go back.

Back through four watershed UPS transitions: synchronizing global commerce, achieving the biggest and fastest airline start-up in history, popularizing common carrier service, and delivering retail products for urban department stores. Backing through time, you catch glimpses of a company paralyzed by a strike in the 1990s, blindsided by more energetic competition in the 1970s, battling with the U.S. government in the 1960s, reeling on the ropes with a dead business model in the early 1950s, and mired in the Depression's woeful economics in the 1930s.

Soon you find yourself all the way back—100 years to be exact—to 1907 Seattle, when a tiny company called the American Messenger Company was started by a teenager named Jim Casey. And this is what you find out about UPS and the nature of change.

1

The "Big Idea": Culture as Competitive Advantage

"Anybody can deliver packages—from the small boy in the neighborhood on up to the most extensive delivery systems in the land. The one thing we can have to offer that others will not always have is quality."

—JIM CASEY, *UPS Founder,*
Plant Managers Conference, 1946

THE WILD WEST

A full decade after the first gold discoveries in the Klondike, thousands of rough-and-ready travelers poured into Seattle in 1907, lured by the promise of riches in the American West.

Jim Casey knew better than most about seeking one's fortune. The nineteen-year-old had just returned to Seattle from two years immersed in the frenzy of Goldfield, Nevada, a boomtown characterized in a 1905 *Los Angeles Times* article as the best place in the world for "a poor man to become rich and a rich man to become poor." Casey had become neither richer nor poorer in Goldfield, but had instead furthered his education into just how much labor and downright danger his ambition to build a messenger service business could entail.

True, gold fever made for good customers, men with a little money who periodically received mail, telephone and telegraph messages, and parcels. But trouble often announced itself with these fortune-seekers as well, in the form of ubiquitous prostitutes, readily available opium and cocaine, and vicious fighting. Even before setting out for Goldfield as a seventeen-year-old in 1905, however, Casey's experiences as a Seattle messenger had likely caused him to shed any illusions he held about the dark side of human nature.

One of four children, Casey was born on March 29, 1888, in Candelaria, Nevada, and moved to Seattle with his family when he was eight. Destined by circumstance and a sickly father to quit school at age eleven and earn money, he worked as a messenger for a department store, a tea store, and a telegraph company before partnering at age fifteen with two other messengers to launch their own business. The teenage Casey soon learned, as his later writings put it, how "the night half of the world lived." One evening he might find himself collecting bail money for prisoners; the next buying "cocaine and morphine from drug stores for dope fiends . . . [and] opium from Chinese for use by opium-smokers, sometimes called 'hop-heads.' "

For the more respectable citizens of Seattle, Casey delivered telegrams, mail, and packages; hauled luggage to and from the train station; carried meals from the city's best restaurants to diners in hotels and boarding houses; and even provided babysitting for parents attending the opera or theater. Seattle's geography helped make messengers a particularly popular brand of service providers. The city's steep hills, some at a twenty-percent gradient, even prompted members of the Seattle Symphony in the late 1800s to rig a pulley system to haul tubas and other instruments, lest the wind instrument players be too winded to perform.

Casey's early experience with Seattle's nocturnal bacchanalia served as an audition of sorts for Goldfield, where Casey would encounter a literal case of "killing the messenger." After a huge mine near Goldfield in 1902 became more and more legendary for the riches it held, Casey and one partner closed their Seattle messenger service and headed out in 1905 to the dry hills east of the Sierras, where thousands of others had already converged on Goldfield.

But by early 1905 all of the claims with any potential had been taken. According to one prospector's comments in a 1905 *Los Angeles Times* article, "The men who have come to Goldfield expecting to stake claims . . . are up against a hard proposition. For sixty miles around, all the available land is staked." When the partners realized they had arrived too late to join the prospectors, they decided to set up a messenger service.

Population estimates for Goldfield in 1906 run as high as 30,000, most jammed into a cluster of ramshackle buildings. Information in the camp traded at a premium. "The post office, telegraph and telephone offices were crowded far into the night," a historian of Goldfield noted. Moreover, ". . . Throughout the day, messengers were sent to the principal hotels and saloons to call out the names of persons for whom messages were being held."

Casey and his partner quickly homed in on one particular

niche in the town's information network. Goldfield's six hundred telephones all connected through a single switchboard. The partners struck a deal with the telephone office manager: they would deliver the exchange's messages for a monthly fee of fifty dollars, along with use of a corner of the office for any additional business they managed to drum up on their own. They bought bicycles, and the business was off and running, or rather, pedaling.

Hotels, saloons, and brothels proliferated in Goldfield. The most well known was the Northern, owned by Tex Rickard, later a famous boxing promoter and owner of Madison Square Garden in New York City. For Goldfield, the Northern was hugely impressive in scale, featuring a massive, elongated bar so big that during peak hours eighty men were required to tend it. On Labor Day 1906, Rickard staged the world lightweight boxing championship in Goldfield, pitting reigning champion Joe Gans of Baltimore against Battling Nelson of Denmark.

According to contemporary newspaper reports, more than 10,000 of Goldfield's gold-searching, pleasure-seeking residents gathered to watch the fight. In the chaotic days after the forty-two-round bout that one spectator described as "the greatest lightweight championship bout ever contested," Casey's partner was on his bike making a delivery just outside the Northern, when he collided with "one of the disreputable characters of the town." Enraged, the man pulled a gun and shot the teenager dead.

On top of it all, Casey contracted a severe case of typhoid and a doctor recommended he'd be better off in a sea-level climate. It was back to Seattle, and the drawing board, for Casey.

A THIRD TRY IN SEATTLE

When Casey returned to Seattle, he found it in the midst of its own full-court press to lure prospective millionaires to Seattle for supplies before embarking to the Klondike. Prospectors were encouraged to spend the winter months in Seattle as well.

Seattle not only had the natural advantage of being the northernmost major American railroad stop, it had in native son Erastus Brainerd, the head of the Seattle Chamber of Commerce, an indefatigable public relations genius who did anything he could to associate Seattle with Alaska.

In the name of the Chamber of Commerce, Brainerd wrote to governors, mayors, and members of Congress from all over the country, cautioning that they must send their fortune-seeking constituents to Seattle to get properly outfitted for the travails ahead. He took out advertisements in all the major Eastern publications of the day, among them the *New York Journal, Scribner's, Harper's Weekly,* and *McClure's.* Before long, the *Cheechakos,* an Alaskan pejorative for "tenderfoot," headed for Seattle for their jumping-off point to Alaska.

Seattle's population grew explosively, swelling from 80,000 in 1900 to more than 230,000 in 1910. Soon, there were more taverns in Seattle than restaurants or stores. The first white settlers of Seattle had called it "New York-Ali," meaning in the local American Indian vernacular "New York by-and-by," and now that characterization seemed like it was coming to pass.

Casey, as stealthily ambitious as Brainerd was self-promoting, would benefit from the traffic as much as anyone, for he was set to launch a new business. But unsavory elements were flourishing in Seattle more than ever, facilitated by a corrupt police chief named Charles Wappenstein, who a few years later would be convicted of taking bribes from owners of brothels and illegal gambling dens. For example, the owner of one messenger company was charged in 1907 with helping to hook six of his messengers on cocaine. Under the man's tutelage the boys had become opium and cocaine "fiends," according to the *Los Angeles Times,* and the city subsequently banned anyone under eighteen from entering saloons or other places of vice, and mandated that all messenger call boxes be located on the exterior of such establishments.

Reacting against all he had seen and experienced over the previous few years—messenger boys addicted to drugs and the cold-blooded murder of a partner among them—Casey and his new partner, Claude Ryan, resolved to employ only clean-cut boys from good families who they knew personally, figuring "only this way could we get reliable boys who would be honest in their dealings with customers." In a roundabout way, then, the buttoned-up, Eagle-Scout earnestness that UPS is so well known for today developed in part as a reaction against the gold-fever–inspired, turbulent times in which Casey first did business.

To house this new business, the partners rented a room with borrowed seed money of one hundred dollars, in the basement of—what else—a saloon, in a part of Seattle's commercial district called Pioneer Square, a section of town teeming with immigrants and thriving on trade with the Far East. For furniture, the fledgling firm installed an old, discarded "free-lunch" counter and a bench on which messengers would sit between calls. Two telephones, one for each of Seattle's telephone companies, and a new bicycle completed the partner's assets. The American Messenger Company was born.

The company stayed open all night and on Sundays, even though Casey, Ryan, and their messengers often ended up twiddling their thumbs with little to do. Casey reasoned that this was the surest way to earn the American Messenger Company a reputation for dependability.

THE ORIGINS OF CULTURE AT UPS

Seattle already had eight or nine messenger companies when Casey and Ryan opened their shop. To differentiate themselves, they would have to price their services competitively, work harder, and deliver better service than their competitors. The two American Messenger Service partners had placards printed to market the promise of BEST SERVICE—LOWEST RATES. Much of the company's early business came from delivering Western Union telegrams, which in 1907 completely dominated the telegraph business. Western Union operated more than 1,500 miles of wire and, out of the more than 100 million telegraph messages sent in the U.S in 1907, it facilitated almost seventy-five million of them.

In 1913 Casey and Ryan merged their venture with another small Seattle delivery business run by a young man named Evert McCabe. McCabe was cut from the same cloth as Casey. He attended the University of Washington but left school early to become a messenger, and he also was an inveterate entrepreneur. By joining forces with McCabe, the company gained not only employees—McCabe's company was up to thirty—but added several motorcycles, which were fast growing in popularity in the United States.

The company's first motorized vehicles were welcome in that they made negotiating Seattle's hills a little easier. But McCabe also brought an expansive sense of optimism and strategic vision that would make him one of the most important figures at UPS for many years. "A characteristic of his," former UPS CEO Paul Oberkotter once wrote, "was to build a big idea out of a glimmer of a dream." McCabe and Casey soon became the two guiding forces behind the company: Casey, the reflective businessman, McCabe, the enthusiastic dreamer.

UNDER THE RADAR SCREEN WITH A NEW KIND OF DELIVERY SERVICE

McCabe's arrival precipitated a pivotal strategic decision. Up to that point, the services provided by the American Messenger Company were not any more sophisticated than what Casey was doing years earlier in his smaller messenger businesses. Once McCabe came on board, the firm adopted the name Merchants Parcel Delivery, and began to focus on deliveries for small retail businesses in downtown Seattle.

Just as Casey had found an unfilled niche in Goldfield, he and his partners had now found their own market, one that presented the opportunity of real, sustainable growth. Local delivery between shops and stores and their customers was a service that the so-called Big Four express companies—Adams, American Express, Wells Fargo, and United States Express—had precious little interest in at that time.

The business of the Big Four express companies was moving heavy freight and medium- and small-sized parcels from town to town using trains, steamboats, and stagecoaches. Unlike countries such as the United Kingdom (U.K.) and Germany, there was no parcel post in the United States until 1913, so anything bigger than a letter had to be sent with one of the express companies. For example, all of those supplies that needed to get from Seattle to Nome? These four companies had a hammerlock on that business, running steamships between Alaska and Washington State along the Pacific Coast.

Much as the number of packages handled by UPS and FedEx today is seen as one indicator of national business robustness, the volume of business of the Big Four express companies was then taken as a reliable barometer of the country's economic health. One executive with American Express was quoted in a 1905 *Wall Street Journal* article as saying, "The volume of packages sent by express is always a fair indication of the country and judging from the amount we are handling, there was never such good times."

Of the thirty-four large express companies doing business in the United States in 1908, these four had enormous clout with the government and the railroads; some even called them a cartel because they rarely underpriced one another and effectively blocked the government and other express carriers from getting any of their business. For example, in 1906 the four express companies were the biggest users of the railroad, accounting for more than two percent of total volume on the U.S. railroads. That year, American Express delivered products over 39,000 miles of railroad and maintained 6,000 offices, while Wells Fargo ran goods over 45,000 miles of railroad out of 4,700 offices. The business arrangements between the railroads and the four major express companies, however, were often characterized by disputes about pricing.

American railroads didn't like to get pushed around; they were essentially the first modern corporations in America, and the rise and leverage of the express companies was disturbing to them. The Pennsylvania Railroad, for example, was the first to assume such traits as joint stock, equity, and leadership by professional managers. Other early railroad corporations were the Erie, Baltimore, and Ohio.

Eventually the nature of the relationships between the express companies and the railroads evolved from "one-off" contracts to more long-term arrangements in which the railroads received a percentage of the express company's profits.

It's impossible to know whether Casey had his eyes on the big express players' business at the time because he never mentioned it in his writings. But he knew enough about them to know that they weren't interested in local retail delivery. In fact, they weren't equipped to perform the service because they didn't tend to own their own vehicles.

The local delivery business in 1913, as opposed to the heavy freight express business, was defined in the popular imagination as a coarse, dirty business conducted by teamsters, who were, literally, men who drove wagons powered by teams of horses.

In 1912, a domestic parcel post service was created by Congress, taking effect on January 1, 1913. By prearrangement, the first item sent was a carton of apples, delivered to President-elect Woodrow Wilson's home in Princeton, New Jersey, a few minutes after midnight. Wilson, still New Jersey's governor until heading to the White House in March, was celebrating with his family and signed for the package himself. That same night, parcel post packages were sent from cities all over the country; the first parcel post package sent from Philadelphia was a set of souvenir spoons from the Postmaster General to President Taft, while in Birmingham, Alabama a five-foot pitchfork was the first item sent.

Foreshadowing a service that Casey would soon tap into, the *New York Times* declared the next day that, "Several postmasters have already reported that large department stores and mail order houses in the big cities, such as New York, Chicago, Cincinnati, St. Louis and Boston, have signified their intention of using the parcel post for local deliveries to replace local express companies."

With Casey as the constant, one of the early partners departed from Merchants Parcel Delivery. Ryan withdrew from the business shortly after McCabe arrived and Casey's brother George joined the company. In 1917, the partnership reached what proved to be critical mass when it brought in Charlie Soderstrom, who handled deliveries for Fraser Patterson, one of Seattle's leading department stores. Soderstrom brought in nuts and bolts experience; he knew how to manage fleets and run department store delivery operations. Within a year of Soderstrom's arrival, the company had persuaded three of Seattle's largest department stores to turn over their entire delivery operations.

As Casey would later say, UPS didn't invent the retail delivery business, but it did refine it with improvements that meant better service for customers. For example, delivery from department stores with some couriers could sometimes take days.

Early on, Merchants Parcel realized that it could win a lot of business if it developed a reputation for quick delivery. That meant the package cars couldn't break down, so the company started purchasing premium "India" tires, guaranteed by the manufacturer to last 20,000 miles.

By 1919 the company was looking to expand into other cities further down the West Coast. Oakland was first, in 1919, and from this expansion the partners renamed their company United Parcel Service. Oakland was followed by Los Angeles in 1922, San Francisco in 1925, and Portland, Oregon in 1927. Foreshadowing UPS's struggles to expand nationally from the 1950s through the 1980s, the California State Railroad Commission challenged the rights of UPS to expand to some communities in California. In 1927, UPS was awarded the rights to expand to San Diego and Santa Barbara over objections from the Commission that various local trucking companies would be shut out of serving retailers in those areas.

While UPS strove for anonymity while delivering retail goods— that's generally the way the West Coast department stores liked it—the company wasn't shy about approaching customers. It developed a small sales force with a few professionals in each city it expanded into and even started to advertise in the *Los Angeles Times* about its burgeoning new business. One advertisement highlighting "United's fine-looking brown-and-gold delivery cars" even shows a drawing of Casey smiling out at newspaper readers.

UPS also took pains to contribute economically and socially in other new areas of operation. Thus, in late 1929, when the Los Angeles mayor decided to make a speech on the increasing traffic problems in the city, UPS hosted the mayor at one of its United Parcel Service Breakfast Club events. Because one UPS truck on the road might replace as many as four or five delivery trucks owned by retail stores, UPS offered one small part of the solution to L.A.'s traffic woes.

It's no surprise that UPS had growth on its mind during this time. The period between 1900 and 1920 was a time of tremendous growth for the U.S. economy, when companies that, like UPS, would become premier brands of the twentieth century took hold and prospered, organizations such as General Electric, Kellogg's, Quaker Oats, Colgate, Procter & Gamble, Ford, and Nabisco. During this period entire new industries developed as well, such as the tobacco industry. But these types of companies all dwarfed UPS at this point. Indeed, the company was still concerned with persuading department stores outside of Seattle that it could be trusted to handle their deliveries.

THE POLICY OF SPIC AND SPAN: BECOMING "BROWN"

The department stores were open to the idea of cutting costs, of course. And in theory, UPS's business concept made sense: consolidating the delivery routes that each of a city's various stores operated individually would eliminate duplication and thus yield efficiencies. The proposition amounted to an early twentieth-century version of outsourcing. But the stores were wary about relinquishing control, and protective of the standards of service they set.

Major department stores in large cities in the early 1900s—

establishments like Fraser Patterson in Seattle, The Emporium in San Francisco, or Macy's in New York—prided themselves on the high-end nature of the retail environments and experiences they conjured. After all, this was the age of grand department stores, with lavish marbled lobbies and elegant, bow-tied floor managers.

As UPS began courting these kinds of customers, it had to persuade them that the delivery company would both provide excellent service to customers and reflect well on them.

For a start, there would have to be both a dress code and a code of etiquette. Instilling a professional appearance and attitude among UPS drivers became a pressing strategic imperative as it set its sights on a consolidated delivery business. "Although the company was born in a basement and reared in an alley," Casey would later relate, "early on we made up our minds that we didn't want to be identified as an 'alley company,' as most other delivery companies had been. We early adopted the policy of spic and span appearance for the few delivery cars that we had."

The effort to pull the delivery business out of "the alley" and sell it to department stores made style just as important as substance for UPS by the early 1920s. Behind the scenes, to be sure, the company would have to execute efficiently, mastering the logistics of metropolitan delivery systems. But department stores, and the customers who frequented them, represented a world far removed from the saloons and taverns of Goldfield and Seattle, where messengers were treated badly and, as demonstrated with Casey's partner, even killed.

For these new customers, success hinged on appearance and trust—on *brand*, if you will. For UPS drivers, that meant fresh

shaves, pristine uniforms, no smoking on the job, and scrupu-
lous politeness. It also meant higher pay than at other driving
jobs. UPS "attaches the utmost importance to the type of drivers
employed and the training given them," Casey promised San
Francisco retailers in 1924 in a pitch letter for their business.
"They are paid more than the prevailing scale of wages and are
selected with due regard to their appearance, personality and
manners."

As department store deliveries became the core business, this
attention to detail and concern for professional appearance became a defining aspect of UPS. As UPS began courting the department stores, Soderstrom pushed for a single, uniform color
to replace the yellow and red package cars UPS had in its fleet.
When a friend recommended the color similar to that used
by the Pullman Company on their railroad passenger cars, UPS
adopted the suggestion in 1919. In the mid-1920s, UPS took up
an idea from one of its drivers and installed shoe shine kits and
mirrors in drivers' locker rooms. In 1925, the company began
issuing its drivers standardized brown uniforms in all cities
where the company operated.

Brown worked in part because it was more conservative, yes,
but also because brown package cars looked cleaner on the
roads, and UPS needed its cars looking as "spic and span" as its
drivers. "Keeping vehicles and equipment in such fine condition that they look even better than new trucks out of the factory is one of Mr. Soderstrom's hobbies which he rides hard,"
the trade journal *Motor Transport* reported in 1924 after touring
UPS facilities. Washers cleaned every package car each night,
and, once each week, steamed and cleaned the inside of the vehicles and varnished and touched up the outside.

AN IDENTIFIABLE CORPORATE CULTURE

In the firm's early years, the work of forging culture was relatively straightforward. A collective commitment to ways of doing business, and in particular an appreciation for maintaining impeccable standards of service, could be conveyed by example. The founders knew their employees personally. Everybody worked alongside one another, shoulder to shoulder. The partners' origins as messenger boys and deliverymen was living, breathing proof that the company could be successful.

Beginning with the move to Oakland in 1919, however, the challenges of management grew more complicated. In order to expand, the company needed to fold in new people and set up new operations hundreds of miles away. The move into Los Angeles three years later only broadened those challenges.

Enforcing UPS standards in these new operations was the easy part. The harder test was conveying what the uniforms and freshly painted cars stood for. In Oakland, Los Angeles, and San Francisco, no less than Seattle, UPS would rely on its drivers, plant managers, and supervisors to set a tone of business that would attract and keep department stores and other retailers as customers.

But for what UPS wanted to accomplish in these new markets, it couldn't rely on example and word of mouth alone. In 1922, UPS started to communicate to potential customers through direct mail advertising. The company hired a Los Angeles–based advertising agency called Mayers to write and design sales literature that could help convince wholesalers and retailers to hire UPS to deliver their products. It even let the company place an ad in newspapers using UPS as an example of how it could produce campaigns for "Hard to Advertise" businesses.

UPS also looked for ways to reinforce the cultural ties binding the organization together. In 1924 it began publishing a company newsletter called the *Big Idea*. With this innovation, UPS was one of just a few at the forefront of business communications in the U.S., along with companies like National Cash Register. A year earlier the *Kiplinger Letter*, still one of the most widely read business forecasting newsletters, was launched, but internal corporate newsletters didn't really gain traction until the 1930s.

As a company publication, the *Big Idea* certainly reflected the outlook of senior management. But it spoke in an open, informal tone, solicited anecdotes, tips, and other contributions from drivers, and invited UPSers in general into dialog with one another. The *Big Idea* quickly found an organic voice that articulated a living sense of mission and shared opportunity.

From its earliest issues, the *Big Idea* bombarded UPS's drivers with sermons, suggestions, and stories that relentlessly reiterated the point that the existence of the modern business enterprise was to serve customers. Typical of UPS culture, nothing was too small to be addressed in the *Big Idea*, which reminded drivers not to smoke or open the door of a customer's home while delivering a package.

One can hear the echoes in UPS today. The same basic message, by now etched into the psyche of the organization, reiterates itself in the pre-work communications meetings held every morning in UPS facilities around the world. The message is the same that earlier generations of UPS drivers received: drivers remain the public face of UPS, as much in Shanghai and Istanbul as Boston or Atlanta.

THE ORIGINS OF THE OWNERSHIP COMPANY

In 1927, with the West Coast phase of expansion in hand and the firm's leadership laying plans for even more ambitious moves, the founding partners sent letters to fifty-two UPSers inviting them to become part owners of the company, one of the first stock-offering plans in American business. Specifically, the founders offered designated employees a chance to purchase "Associates' Shares" that gave full voting rights and dividend privileges. In real, substantial terms, the partners were restructuring UPS to make it a much wider partnership.

A few other companies did offer employees equity opportunities in various forms before UPS; Procter & Gamble instituted a profit-sharing plan in 1887 and Kodak instituted wage-sharing in 1912. But what was distinctive about UPS's plan was that it went beyond basic profit-sharing to actual voting shares. The Procter & Gamble and Kodak programs only evolved into stock-offering plans later.

Because the news went out in late December, the *Big Idea* described the offer as "probably the most valuable Christmas present ever received" by the selected recipients. Shares were offered at fifteen dollars each, and recipients were given five years to pay.

The breadth of the offer was generous. With nearly 500 UPSers in 1927, the founders were extending equity to more than one-tenth of the employees. From then on, the company's owners would include not just executives but front-line employees, too. By 1936, the company's shareholder base would number 602 employee owners, including 247 drivers and helpers, as well as sixty-eight mechanics, washers, and porters.

The extension of equity was a shrewd business move, as well. The founders had been weighing the idea and collecting advice on how to restructure the firm along these lines "for several years," Casey told the firm's bankers when he informed them of the move. The founders were not extending equity because they needed financial capital. Instead, it was *human* capital they were after. UPS needed commitment and faith and a level of performance from their people that would go well beyond a typical, corporate employer-employee relationship. They needed heart. The goal behind the new policy, Casey explained in a letter to the credit agency Bradstreet, was to invest the company's people "in the building of its business."

Ultimately, the founders of UPS decided to make their business an ownership company because they recognized the need to demonstrate that they really did believe what they had been preaching, namely, that UPS's long-term strategic success depended on its people. By relinquishing a share of equity, they were daring employees to put some skin in the game.

PROMOTION FROM WITHIN

Inviting UPSers to become partners in name as well as in spirit certainly lent substance and credibility to the pitch. Creating opportunity for advancement within the organization played an equally formative role—both in encouraging UPSers and in fortifying internal cohesion. By 1930, promoting from within was becoming bedrock UPS policy.

The promote-from-within policy wasn't ironclad, just as it isn't today. After UPS bought some Remington typewriters for its Los Angeles office in 1923 to help process CODs more efficiently and speed up bookkeeping, Casey decided some accountants were needed on staff to make the most of the new technology. George Smith was recruited from the accounting firm of E. L. Barette in 1925 after Casey noticed his quiet tenaciousness and facile understanding of the business model UPS had developed. Smith would eventually succeed Casey as CEO in 1962.

Necessity played a part in the formation of the promote-from-within philosophy, because the company was expanding at a breakneck pace. Late in the 1920s, as UPS continued to expand, it was inevitable that Casey would turn to the skies. Himself an entrepreneur and seeker of adventure, as evidenced from his time in Goldfield, Casey had often talked to colleagues about the strong impression the 1903 Wright Brothers' flights in Kitty Hawk, North Carolina, had made on him. Then came Lindbergh's transatlantic flight in May 1927.

Granted, in the late 1920s passenger flight was still a novelty (though a company named Maddux Air Lines operated five passenger routes on the West Coast, three through Los Angeles), but several private couriers were already running profitable businesses delivering packages and mail through the air. In 1925, a company called Western Air Express, for example, started carrying parcels between Los Angeles and Salt Lake City, at a cruising speed of about 120 miles an hour.

In October 1926, A. K. Humphries of the Pacific Air Transport said that 300,000 letters and parcels were sent through the air that month, an increase of 8 percent over the previous month. So, true to form, UPS didn't invent the service, but came around quickly to realize attractive economies of scale. In Feb-

ruary 1929, even as UPS contemplated its coming launch of operations in New York City, the company launched United Air Express, an air delivery service linking UPS's West Coast operations and customers.

With Los Angeles as the "hub," the service covered major cities on the Pacific Coast and as far east as Texas. In addition to Los Angeles, stops included Seattle; Portland; San Francisco; Oakland; Medford, Oregon; San Diego; Imperial, Arizona; Phoenix; Tucson; and El Paso. Casey's plan was to link all of these cities and beat out companies like Western Air Express by providing stops at more destinations more frequently. Piggybacking on the aforementioned passenger service, the planes UPS used could carry four people and a limited number of packages, but enough to be profitable if the cargo hold was filled.

Unfortunately, the timing for the new venture couldn't have been worse. Eight months after the air express service launched, the stock market crashed. Just over a week after the stock market crash, though, UPS apparently still had high hopes for its air ambitions, and even announced, according to the November 7, 1929 edition of the *Wall Street Journal*, a coast-to-coast air freight service that would take forty hours from Los Angeles to New York. Eastbound traffic would consist of silk from Asia and fresh California fruit and vegetables, while going back West, various kinds of manufactured merchandise would fill the hold.

Given the business conditions, though, United Air Express couldn't generate enough packages to fill the West Coast routes, much less realize the vision of the West Coast–East Coast runs. In April 1931, as business conditions continued to spiral downward and the Great Depression squeezed the economy, UPS shuttered the venture.

The fact that the onset of the Great Depression killed the air express idea in its infancy did not change the fact that expanding to New York weighed heavily on Casey's mind. Starting operations in New York, the largest commercial marketplace in the country, would double the size of UPS, triple its volume, and quadruple its geographic scope. Besides subjecting the idea to the detailed due diligence that every new operation had to undergo—assuring sufficient delivery volume potential, canvassing department stores, researching the acquisitions of a going delivery concern—the company also had to consider what the economic downturn would do to its business.

Eventually it plunged ahead. What's remarkable is that UPS was committed to national growth even while American business was spiraling down toward its nadir. The company, in fact, would grow from 650 employees in 1932 to 1,650 employees in 1934, many of these people being hired to work in New York at UPS's facility at 38th Street and First Avenue.

A month after the expansion, the *Big Idea* touted the benefits of working for UPS to the new employees, saying that promotion from within the ranks was "one of the major policies of the United Parcel Service, and that practically every executive at the company started at the bottom." Soon enough, the New York operation showed that the company was as good as its word, promoting three local drivers, an assistant, several dispatchers, and a cashier to supervisor and management positions. At the same time, UPS had no trouble quickly gaining its first big New York customers: Lord & Taylor, Hahne's, and James McCreery & Co.

THE "POLICY BOOK": A DIFFERENT KIND OF CORPORATE COMMUNICATIONS

Policies of all kinds were firming up by the late 1920s. Not co-incidentally, UPS leaders were beginning to articulate company values and management principles in formal terms. Characteristically, the company's leadership was approaching the process methodically and self-consciously, consulting one another along the way, gathering consensus, and trying to capture, in writing, what was working. Expansion, for Casey and company, was always an occasion for reflection and self-examination.

In June 1928, Jim Casey wrote to a wide range of UPS's managers soliciting ideas about why UPS had been successful. The responses, collated and culled by both Casey and his brother, became a document UPS called the "Policy Book." The current version is still the company's bible today and is read and discussed at the start of staff meetings in UPS offices all over the world.

Assembling the "Policy Book" was a pet project that Casey nurtured lovingly. Part business plan, part employee handbook, part mission statement, the "Policy Book" captured what was by now coalescing as the essence of UPS. Casey's inspiration for the book might have come from CEO peers, customers, or colleagues, but if other companies had such a document at that time, no one has revealed it.

Capturing and codifying company values, the "Policy Book" carried declarations such as: "Every worker in this business must be given a square deal. . . . In all of our dealings with our people, we must be careful not to show favoritism."

The effort to put the "Policy Book" together revealed a great deal about the kind of enterprise UPS was becoming. And above all, it revealed an extraordinary commitment to what today goes by the name of culture.

THE MARK OF THE FOUNDER

Through those first twenty-five years at UPS, Jim Casey experienced enormous success in business but personal tragedy as well. Co-founder Evert McCabe was shot and killed in 1933 by his mentally ill wife who was distraught over the death of their twenty-two-year-old son, Gene, two years earlier. Charlie Soderstrom was freakishly hit and disabled by a golf ball.

Yet during the first twenty-five years of the company, UPS share prices never decreased in value—not even by a penny. In fact, in the very midst of the Depression, Casey, speaking before a state railroad commission on November 3, 1932, said that UPS made up "the largest parcel delivery service which has been developed in the history of the world." It was unlike UPS or Casey to trumpet this fact, but it was true. The company was now moving 10 million packages each year and the formerly dominant express companies had been waylaid by their inability to adapt. By 1934, in the New York area alone, UPS made deliveries for more than 250 stores. For the week ending December 15, 1934, for example, the company's retail deliveries had gone up 19 percent from the same week the previous year.

UPS was thriving and Casey believed, as he later wrote, that it had to do with "getting the best people possible." But it all started with him and the management techniques he espoused, such as promoting from within, the stock ownership plan, and the real interest executives showed in employees' progress—all of which has left an indelible stamp on the enterprise. UPS is most decidedly a company with a founding father. Every CEO since Casey has found reasons to invoke his spirit, whether to remind UPSers of enduring truths or to prepare them for new challenges.

Indeed, Casey is a presence that past and current UPS managers reference and "consult" often. To take just one of many examples, former CEO Jim Kelly took the occasion of his retirement speech to reflect on the reasons for UPS's successful growth into a global corporation. Kelly argued that the company had grown and prospered because UPS recognized that, "Culture matters. A strong, distinct, and unapologetic corporate culture is not something we should run from. Rather, it's something we should embrace." And that awareness, in turn, Kelly attributed to Casey. In Kelly's words, "Our willingness to emulate the principles and standards of our founder, Jim Casey, has guided UPS through the years."

Casey might have protested at that point. He habitually tried to deflect attention from himself when talking about UPS. When *The New Yorker* profiled the company in 1947, the writer, Philip Hamburger, wrote Casey requesting some personal background. Casey obliged reluctantly, offering an autobiographical account up to 1907 but then insisting: "From this point on, remember that the story is to be about *us*—not about me. For in simple fairness to the many capable people who in the intervening years have been associated with the company, no single individual should be given a disproportionate share of credit for the development of the United Parcel Service."

A dynamic founder can be an invaluable asset for a young

company, but a problematic legacy as well. Every company has to eventually outgrow its origins and move beyond the vision, energy, ethos, and outlook that set it in motion. Casey, to his credit, saw this test coming and worked doubly hard to instill UPS with the cultural outlook, leadership talent, and management tools to survive it. That may well have been the biggest idea within the Big Idea.

2

Constructive Dissatisfaction and the Quest for Continuous Improvement

"You are far more interested in improving what is bad than in crowing about what is good. You are constructively dissatisfied."

—JIM CASEY, *UPS founder, "A Talk with Joe,"*
UPS Management Conference, 1956

WORKING THE NIGHT SHIFT AT WORLDPORT

Around 11 P.M. the last passenger flights disappear into the evening sky, the ticket agents go home, and the taxi lines dissipate. Oddly enough, that's when things really begin to get interesting at Louisville's international airport.

UPS, in close cooperation with Louisville's city fathers, has carved out a large piece of the airport's cargo facilities, called Worldport, for its global air express hub. Every minute or two between 11:30 P.M. and 2 A.M. at Worldport, a UPS-owned or -leased aircraft—the company uses MD-11s, 757s, 767s, 747s, Airbus A300s, even Lear jets—lands on a runway. On a typical night, more than 100 UPS planes from all around the world converge on Worldport. With UPS as its biggest cargo customer, Louisville ranked fourth in cargo handled at U.S. airports in 2005.

Between 11:30 P.M. and 5 A.M., UPS unloads, sorts, and reloads onto the outgoing Browntails (UPS lingo for its air fleet) somewhere between 800,000 and one million domestic and international air packages. By dawn, the fleet will be airborne, planes weighed down once again with the stuff of world trade. UPS calls this drill the sort, and it constitutes one of the marvels of modern commerce.

Worldport, occupying four million square feet, four floors, three concourses bristling with forty-four aircraft docks, and staffed by more than 5,000 UPS night owls, dramatically displays UPS's operational and engineering genius. Although UPS announced in May 2006 that Worldport will undergo a $1 billion expansion to increase capacity, the heart of the facility will remain a series of massive interconnected buildings where the sorting is actually done, although the term "done" implies a level of expended human effort that is unneeded here. Once the igloo-like containers, roughly the size of compact cars, are unloaded, packages are touched just twice by human hands— once at the beginning and once at the end of the sort.

THE SORT

The process of sorting begins almost instantly once workers place the packages on the belts. Using a sorting technology first developed by UPS in Germany during the 1990s for its Frankfurt ground sorting hub, parcels and boxes of every shape and size enter a densely woven architecture of automated ramps, conveyor belts, and bins. Infrared scanners begin reading bar codes and the smaller dots and whorls of UPS's smart labels, as packages—small, regulars, and "irregs," or oddly shaped parcels—ride the first set of belts into the system.

Within seconds, mechanical blocks of rubber that look like big hockey pucks begin shunting packages onto other dipping and diving belts, channeling the packages through a computer-calculated labyrinth of 120 miles of conveyor belts. The approximately two-mile journey of a typical package along Worldport's conveyors takes about thirteen minutes before it emerges in an outgoing bin, routed for one of the igloos heading back out into the Kentucky night.

At various vistas within Worldport, a visitor not vulnerable to vertigo can glimpse packages as they travel single file through the system in all four directions like cars racing through a thread of busy freeways. To keep Worldport's flow moving smoothly, a central database monitors some fifty-nine million transactions every hour, directing packages along optimized paths through the system.

Worldport is also a study in how UPS achieves its stated mission of synchronizing commerce, a goal written on the side of every package car. The company handles more than fifteen million packages around the world each day, and every one must be scanned and routed through the company's global network. This feat is accomplished by taking advantage of simple geography. The strategically chosen Louisville is on the very western edge of the East Coast time zone, placing Worldport as close to the West Coast as possible but also, because of the three-hour time difference, giving UPS the maximum amount of time to process air packages heading west.

Worldport could not have been built in Louisville without the cooperation of the city, the Louisville Regional Airport Authority, the Commonwealth of Kentucky, and the Federal Aviation Administration (FAA). The FAA relocated the airport's original air traffic control tower to better suit UPS's Worldport blueprint. UPS also benefits from a ready pool of part-time labor in the students from the nearby University of Louisville. But Louisville owes UPS just as much, with the company being one of the city's biggest employers and greatly increasing the city's tax base. UPS has also been conscientious about being a good neighbor.

This philosophy goes well beyond the millions of dollars UPS pours into local charitable organizations. In September 2004, for example, it launched—in association with Boeing, the FAA, and MIT—Continuous Descent Approach (CDA), a procedure to help reduce the noise levels in communities near the airport. Using CDA, UPS planes remain at a cruising altitude until very near Louisville, and then make a steeper approach into Worldport. Not only does CDA reduce noise, but it lessens fuel burn and aircraft emissions as well.

CONTINGENCY TEAMS IN THE WINGS

Not all of the 5,000-plus employees who work a night shift at Worldport are down in the sort, of course; some prepare for potential snafus. Every night from Monday to Friday at 7:00 P.M., for example, a dozen or so UPS managers file into a conference room at the Air Service Center for the evening's "hot crew" conference call. Hot crews are stand-by crews waiting to be deployed on a contingency basis wherever snags or glitches erupt in the company's air network.

Along with a systems operation supervisor, the meeting pulls in at least one flight crew member from each of the major aircraft types that UPS flies. Other crews call in from various UPS air hubs in Ontario, California; Philadelphia; Columbia, South Carolina; Dallas; and Rockford, Illinois.

The team is then briefed by the global operations center, also located at Worldport, which monitors incidents or developments that can potentially interrupt the flow of traffic: foul weather, diverted air traffic, or mechanical problems.

Passenger airlines are prone to similar setbacks, as any frequent traveler discovers. A grounded passenger flight might frustrate fifty, seventy-five, or—at the very most—200 or 300 customers. But the delays that constitute business as usual for a passenger airline are unacceptable to UPS. A grounded Brown-tail with a full cargo hold delays some 12,000 packages, and because those parcels involve customers on both the sending and receiving ends, that translates into 24,000 affected customers.

"When we have a disconnect, we feel pain," affirms Rick Barr, a pilot and vice president of UPS Airlines operations. "In the back of your plane, you may have 10,000, 12,000 customers. Now, they're not talking to you like a human passenger, but they are, in a sense, customers. It could be somebody's wedding gown in one package and medical supplies in another."

Keeping a dozen or so crew members and maybe twenty aircraft on call every weekday is an expensive necessity, particularly for an enterprise as focused on the bottom line as UPS. But if there is one thing to understand about UPS, it's that every plan has a back-up plan, and that every back-up plan has a back-up plan. It is, simply, the cost of doing business.

ACHIEVING "SOMETHING THAT HAD NEVER BEEN DONE BEFORE"

While components of Worldport are indeed groundbreaking, UPS's founders offered little that was innovative when first launching the American Messenger Company. But that would soon change in the realms of engineering systems, operating networks, and providing superior customer service.

Once the leaders of the company settled on consolidated delivery as a strategy, they realized that it was going to take a heretofore unattainable level of operational expertise to succeed. The company needed to learn as much as it could about the business it was targeting, and went about gathering information in a disarmingly uncomplicated fashion. UPS management wrote to the chambers of commerce of any U.S. city with a population of over 100,000 and asked for the names of any businesses engaged in consolidating deliveries of retail stores. Obtaining over 100 names, UPS then wrote to all of them.

The replies were not particularly encouraging. Despite the theoretical soundness of the concept, no firms on the West Coast had managed to put together a profitable business. As the superintendent of one San Francisco department store would later explain, the logistical difficulties were formidable. "Right here in San Francisco, in the last fifteen years, I have witnessed no fewer than five failures to run a private delivery system. It looks so easy you know—just take the parcels from your customers, deliver them, and pocket your fee. But to deliver a great volume of parcels with a minimum of loss and breakage, to maintain good schedules and avoid delays, to maintain harmony between the stores and their customers—all this requires a high degree of organization, both in personnel and equipment."

Casey and his partners heard the same basic message: There existed no blueprint for this kind of business. To make the idea work at a level that would sustain customer confidence, they would need to develop new methods. Or as Casey himself put it: "If we were to make a success of the parcel delivery business, we would have to put into it something that had never been done before."

Discovering little in the way of new methodologies within the industry, UPS looked to other industries and businesses, and, despite the company's promote-from-within policy, it also searched far and wide for industrial engineers outside the organization with experience in newly introduced notions of optimizing efficiency. The pioneer in studying industrial processes was Fredrick Taylor, who initiated the scientific management school of thought, and while Taylor had not written anything about UPS's business per se, the company eventually found someone versed in these breakthrough concepts.

His name was Russel Havighorst, and in 1923 UPS invited him into the company to become assistant delivery supervisor. Havighorst was an industrial engineer who had worked with both General Motors and Ford a few years earlier when those companies were learning the basics of assembly line mass production techniques.

He went right to work, studying UPS's package delivery operations and then designing new equipment to streamline the package flow at the company's Los Angeles sorting facility. For example, instead of the customary large, partitioned, crescent-shaped tables sorting was typically done on, Havighorst installed a specially designed belt conveyor and bin system, manned by sorters who sent packages down wooden chutes to bins organized by drivers' routes. At first, the apparatus was "new and strange, making more of a hindrance than an aid," according to the *Big Idea*. But once employees learned how to operate the system, packages began to flow more smoothly through the Los Angeles plant.

Within a year, Havighorst was adapting and installing a modified system for the San Francisco plant and, in place of wooden chutes, installed steel wire chutes with adjustable shelving that allowed for modular construction and modification. Also in San Francisco, the company started equipping its package cars with interior steel cages, allowing handlers to wheel loads into and out of the cars.

AN INDUSTRIAL ENGINEERING ROAD TRIP

This was progress, but UPS was still a young pup when it came to industrial engineering. Casey decided to undertake a further search for ideas, techniques, processes, and technologies that could be adapted to UPS's business. He tackled it personally, hitting the road with Havighorst in 1926 on a tour of the era's leading industrial operations.

The pair traveled widely across the midwestern United States, Canada, and the Atlantic seaboard. Everywhere along the way,

Casey and Havighorst visited department stores and inspected their delivery operations, collecting useable ideas. In Chicago, for example, Casey dismissed Marshall Field's product handling system as being more fit for the "dark ages," but they did pick up ideas about how a large number of packages can be handled by the use of many belts.

Marshall Field's delivery operations were also instructive. While the pair had read much of Field's sorting and delivery system beforehand, the two men marveled at the nine-belt sorting system and 3,500 trunks in which the parcels were stored. Worldport, anyone?

Throughout the trip, Casey and Havighorst took notes, sketched layouts and machinery, and ran calculations about resources spent and time and money saved. One of the most beneficial stops on the tour came at Sears Roebuck, then still a massive and hugely successful mail order company based in Chicago. "We can only touch upon the wonders at Sears Roebuck," Havighorst later wrote. "The success of their entire operation may be said to be due to ideals of the very highest order reinforced by an iron-clad time schedule which holds everyone as strictly to its limitations as those of the old German Imperial army."

Casey and Havighorst also toured Ford's already legendary River Rouge Plant in Michigan, though with Model T production winding down and Model A production not yet in full swing, Havighorst noted that the idle assembly lines gave the facility a palpably gloomy air. In Pittsburgh they stopped at U.S. Steel's mills, and the efficiency illustrated at an Armour meatpacking plant in St. Louis convinced them that even Henry Ford would be impressed. But at American Railway Express, the pair left disappointed and "disgusted" at the crude methods used to keep track of schedules and such items.

Casey and Havighorst were, in fact, engaged in a very rigorous—and a very modern—benchmarking study. Like the Japanese managers who visited American auto plants—and UPS—during the 1950s or modern companies that use management consultant "scorecards" to grade their operations, they wanted to experience and learn from, first-hand, the most innovative practitioners in industry.

THE BIRTH OF CONSTRUCTIVE DISSATISFACTION

Upon returning, Casey was determined that UPS would improve based on what he and Havighorst had learned. Work began immediately on a new conveyor system derived from what they'd seen at Marshall Field's, and when implemented at the Los Angeles Central Division plant in 1928, it wove together nine separate belts and nearly 3,000 feet of belting along a central conveyor 175 feet long.

The technical dimensions and specifications of the Los Angeles conveyor system may not sound particularly impressive today. Certainly anything Havighorst built would be dwarfed in both scale and complexity by later generations of UPS sorting systems. But what was more important than any specific size or scale was the emergence of the industrial engineering ethos that would define the company for the next eight decades. "This highly organized system," explained a business journalist touring the company's plants in 1926, "didn't spring into existence full-grown. It is the fruit of a long, slow process of experimentation and evolution."

Casey and Havighorst, like all of UPS's top managers from those early years, thought in terms of maps, systems, flow, and operational efficiency. They held regular engineering meetings attended by senior managers, all of whom tossed in ideas, questions, and suggestions. At conventions or conferences in hotels, they compulsively sketched out equipment designs and plant layouts on napkins or hotel stationery and passed them around. And they thought not in terms of permanent blueprints but, instead, processes that could be mixed, matched, taken apart, and reassembled.

Jim Casey coined a term to describe this compulsive habit of tinkering with the status quo: "constructive dissatisfaction," which managers actively encouraged. In 1937, for example, the issue was fleet maintenance efficiency. Other years it was the efficacy of electric delivery cars in urban environments, the potential of moving packages by the New York City subway system, or the possible conversion to a monorail-based sort system. UPS engineers tested all these ideas rigorously and quantitatively, always factoring in not just the mechanical efficiencies to be gained, but how the systems would work in the hands of flesh-and-blood employees.

MAKING IT IN NEW YORK

With a population of seven million in 1930, the New York City market was larger than any of UPS's existing markets. The metropolis's major department stores, moreover, were vast commercial hives, dwarfing anything in Seattle, San Francisco, or Los Angeles. Macy's alone did a towering $80 million in sales in 1930 and dispatched 46 million packages that year from the company's palatial New York City store. Consider it this way: Taking on deliveries for Macy's alone would more than double UPS's scale of operations.

Occupying over two million square feet of floor space in Midtown, Macy's maintained a fleet of 436 delivery cars and vans and a force of 900 workers to handle its 35,000 deliveries a day along a network of ninety-six routes. By way of comparison, UPS's entire fleet numbered about 350 trucks and delivery cars in 1928, and a one-day volume of 24,000 packages in 1930 rated as the busiest day for UPS in Los Angeles outside of the Christmas holidays.

And that was just Macy's. A number of smaller department stores did business in New York City, of course, many of them enormous by West Coast standards. The prospect of getting this kind of business was tantalizing for Casey and his team, but it would also stretch UPS well beyond its capacity at the time.

Particularly with its volumes being affected by the Depression, the company needed capital to fuel the expansion to New York. UPS sold some of its stock to outsiders for the first time, and the company's managers actually lost majority ownership of the company before buying it back in 1935. The lesson that Casey and Smith took from that episode and handed down to subsequent generations of UPS managers was never to lose focus on the company's financial condition. Even today, as a public company, UPS's conservative fiscal nature and surplus cash make it one of the few companies in the country with the highest credit rating, Triple A.

In 1930, after protracted negotiations with Lord & Taylor and James McCreery & Co., UPS acquired their joint delivery service. "You sure are playing in the Big Time," an associate wrote to Casey in 1930. Casey agreed. "The combined volume of the three stores which we are already handling is about one and one-half times our total volume at San Francisco," he wrote back.

Both UPS's service culture and its systems-building expertise were put to the test in New York by Gotham's off-the-charts package volume, geographic scale, and complexity of traffic. UPS delivery cars fed loads directly from the department stores into UPS's massive facility on First Avenue, to be sorted and routed out to a network of thirty-two substations located across the New York metropolitan area. As in its West Coast operations, the company sent out two rounds of residential deliveries every day, one in the morning and one in the evening, covering a 50-mile radius.

The labyrinthine central sorting operations foreshadowed Worldport. When *The New Yorker* visited the facility in 1947, it found a hive of activity and an impressively ordered, streamlined flow. Packages ". . . make a series of swift journeys down slides, ramps, chutes and belts. They are put first on an endless rubber belt a hundred feet long, moving at a rate of thirty feet a minute."

To Philip Hamburger, the *New Yorker* reporter, it all seemed at once humdrum—after all, these were packages—and yet, as an operation, somehow elegant and wonderful to behold. Casey, in Hamburger's profile, comes across as vaguely eccentric, even gnome-like. But the writer caught Casey's passion: "Anybody can deliver a package, but our boys know their business and the spokes of our wheel spell *service*! No geniuses. We've got a good idea and it's growing."

UPS IN PERSPECTIVE

Many great companies have come together around a breakthrough product or service or idea. Kodak comes to mind, with the Kodak camera in 1888, and Xerox with its plain paper copier in 1959. AT&T, Microsoft, and Apple offer other cases of companies built around Eureka! events.

UPS, by contrast, represents a different kind of company. It has rarely grown by bursts of pure invention. It has built itself not by inventing so much as by engineering and then reengineering—its equipment, its systems, itself. It joins a tradition epitomized by companies such as IBM, which married world-class sales and marketing and sophisticated computer engineering; and Wal-Mart, which committed to selling goods at the lowest price points possible, and then found ways to do so.

To be sure, the great process companies can innovate. Ford's mass-producible Model T in 1908, IBM's 360 series computers in 1964, and Wal-Mart's linked point-of-sale–inventory systems in the early 1990s are proof of such innovation, along with UPS's development of the consolidated delivery model.

UPS RULES FOR THE ROAD

Constructive Dissatisfaction and the Quest
for Continuous Improvement

- **Create a culture of "constructive dissatisfaction."** This memorable phrase, coined by founder Jim Casey, is all the more effective because it makes the point that continuous improvement is never easy, that it stems from pushing people out of their comfort zones even when things are going great for a business.

- **The little things matter—perhaps most of all.** The bigger a company grows, the more the little things become harder to manage. But it's the unflinching attention to detail that sets a company apart from its competitors. Jim Casey liked to say, "Service is the sum of many little things done well."

3

A Common and Uncommon Carrier: Accomplishing Transformation

*"We can constantly look forward to change. Not change
for change's sake, but for the opportunity to improve."*

—GEORGE SMITH, *UPS CEO, 1962–1972*

THE KING OF WEST 25TH STREET

In the cavernous third-floor parking garage of UPS's main
New York distribution hub at 43rd Street and 12th Avenue on
Manhattan's far west side, Rudy Taylor's brown package car is
packed up and ready to go by 8:45 A.M. The vehicle was washed
during the wee hours, as it is every night before hitting the
road. On this July morning in 2005, 175 or so tightly packed
boxes and envelopes have been loaded, respectable volume for
a Friday in mid-summer.

Taylor, just in from his morning commute from Stamford, Connecticut, reports that the sunrise shift of part-time loaders did
their jobs well: the packages are well-organized by street address,
priority items out in front. UPS employs technology that tells a
loader in which car, on which shelf, and in which position to

place a box or envelope, but those employees who know Taylor and his habits will tweak the placements to fit his preferences.

In addition to the necessary orderliness of the packages, the company's devotion to vehicular precision is also on display. Waves of trucks, staggered at ten-minute intervals, are already snaking their way out of the building via the ramp that winds its way down into the city. Within the next forty-five minutes, a fleet of 400 UPS package cars and tractor trailers will make their way out of the hub.

As he readies to join the rolling brown convoy, Taylor is called back at the last second. A "high-value" item for a customer on Taylor's route—West 25th Street between Sixth and Seventh Avenues—has just come in. UPS defines high-value packages as those worth between $5,000 and $50,000; the company typically won't handle packages valued at more than $50,000 (transporting an iceberg a few years ago proved difficult to place a value on, but that's another story).

People are often surprised to find that UPS handles all sorts of high-ticket items. And because of its proximity to New York's Diamond District on West 45th Street, more high-value items go through the UPS Metro New York District than any other in the world. Security is rigorous and multi-layered.

Drivers on both the pick-up and delivery sides must sign for high-value deliveries, as do the UPS employees who process the items at a sort. Armed guards accompany drivers in the Diamond District, and also escort the trailers full of high-value items out to New York's airports. Technicians whose eyes are glued to consoles use a proprietary software application called the "High Risk Control System" to track the movement of the most valuable deliveries. Taylor's signature now stands as testament that he was the last UPS employee to touch this particular envelope. And if it goes missing after Taylor signs for it? "Let's just say," Taylor says as he maneuvers down the ramp, "losing it is something I'd never even think about."

One of the few perks of a hot, sweaty New York summer day is that Taylor can opt for the casual version of the company's ubiquitous brown uniform. The UPS-logoed golf shirt hanging on Taylor's lean, six-foot-two frame is neatly tucked into belted UPS shorts. A visor, socks, and boots round out Taylor's ensemble.

Like every other driver at UPS facilities around the globe, Taylor must be given the once-over at an 8:30 A.M., three-minute Pre-work Communication Meeting (PCM). Even though UPS is now an enormously complex company with the self-stated mission of "synchronizing global commerce," many business practices that UPS founder Jim Casey introduced decades ago have not only survived into today's company, but indeed flourished. The PCM is one. Taylor will likely never meet UPS drivers like Senol Demircan dodging cars parked in the middle of the street in Istanbul, Patrick De Keersmaecker negotiating European Union meeting traffic in Brussels, or Tom Murphy making deliveries to the Town Hall in small-town Massachusetts. But they all attend PCMs, they all wear brown, and they all further the brand of UPS.

Taylor's supervisor, Jack McCallen, runs the morning PCM and inspects the drivers for pressed uniforms, shined shoes, and close shaves. When McCallen deems the drivers ready to represent UPS, they are ready to venture to their particular corners of the city. "Luckily for me," Taylor says, "my wife presses my shirts and shines my shoes; she wants to make sure I look good."

Taylor will turn fifty-two in December 2007 and has been with UPS for 30 years. Thirty years of negotiating New York City streets, thirty winters of driving in snow and ice, thirty years without so much as a serious fender bender. Five years ago, Taylor was inducted into the Circle of Honor, reserved for those 4,200 UPS drivers with twenty-five years of service without an accident.

Taylor is certainly not alone at UPS as a superb professional driver. Nearly all long-time UPS drivers are exceptional, including the tractor trailer drivers. An armed escort, a former New York City policeman named Frank Bohica, is constantly reminded of how good the UPS rig drivers are as he tails them out to Newark airport or JFK: "Watch this turn," he says to a visitor on a night-time run to Newark. "It's like watching a great artist. Perfect."

As Taylor approaches the intersection of West 44th Street and 11th Avenue, the drivers honk to each other as they disperse in all four directions, easily-overlooked but absolutely critical cogs in the city's daily commerce. The sliding front driver and passenger doors of Taylor's truck are open on the ride downtown, and will be for the rest of the day. "In the '70s and '80s, you couldn't do this," Taylor says, referring to the open-air ride. "People would run right into the truck at a stop light and try to steal your stuff."

As one of UPS's senior drivers, Taylor works one of the most interesting commercial blocks in Chelsea. Wherever quirky entrepreneur/artists dream of striking out on their own, this is surely what they have in mind: floor upon floor of funky graphic design shops, photographic studios, architecture firms, digital cartographers, and musical recording spaces. As Taylor turns on to West 25th Street, his arrival can best be described as a "happening." People stream out of buildings to intercept their packages straight off the truck, like mail call in a war movie. Anonymous, gray Gotham has been transformed into a small village of one block, with Taylor the undisputed mayor for the next eight hours or so.

Taylor pulls over about halfway up the block alongside Apogee U.S.A., sellers of mannequins and "all manners of torsos," at 151 West 25th Street. He parallel parks into a spot marked "Trucks Only." This will be Taylor's base for the day, even though the maximum a commercial vehicle can stay in one spot in New York City is four hours.

Tickets are impossible to avoid for New York City UPS drivers, so there's little incentive for Taylor to move on. Since it's about 9:15 A.M., the day's parking tickets for Taylor and A.B., the UPS driver assigned to the other side of West 25th Street, will likely come at around 1:15 P.M. "He's kind of like us, actually," Taylor says of the officer who usually tickets them. "You can set your watch by him." Could A.B. and Taylor just switch spots after four hours? "It could work," Taylor says. "But I've found that trying to avoid a ticket ends up costing the company more in lost time."

Taylor estimates that he regularly greets upwards of 200 people on West 25th Street each day, and has short interactions with about 100 of them while delivering packages. But what Taylor is really after is a customer signature on his Delivery Information Acquisition Device (DIAD), the hand-held computer that every driver carries to record pickups and deliveries and receive messages from UPS dispatchers. The signature is proof that the package has been delivered safely. As soon as someone signs for a package, that information is uploaded to the mobile messages switch (MMS) at the worldwide technology center in Mahwah, New Jersey. The information is then migrated to another storage device, also in Mahwah, which makes tracking data available to customers, as well as UPS employees.

Initially, Taylor and other UPS drivers weren't all that impressed with the DIAD when it was introduced in 1989. Its performance in the field seemed to confirm every last suspicion of the skeptical drivers, who had been loathe to give up their beloved clipboards. In the first year of deployment, the DIADs experienced a sky-high failure rate of about 40 percent every month. In hot climates the soldering joints melted; in cold climates the face of the DIAD cracked.

There was also the issue that the DIAD only went halfway toward the goal of supplying current information on packages. Because the information collected in the DIAD was transmitted to the company's central package database only once a day, when a driver got back to the sorting facility and uploaded the data, UPS was unable to provide continuous package tracking. After Motorola, the original developer, was brought in to improve the machine, however, the kinks were worked out and drivers soon wondered how they got along without the DIAD.

Among Taylor's deliveries this morning are CDs, cameras, all manner of paper, office equipment from Staples, early cuts of movies and promotional videos, sewing equipment, architectural blueprints, and clothing. When Taylor started on this loop in 1991, the block's proximity to the Garment District, just a little further uptown, used to dictate the business demographics of

West 25th Street and thus the nature of Taylor's deliveries. Back then, Taylor would unload trailers full of sewing machine equipment for American Wigs and other companies. "The big sewing and clothing makers are all gone," Taylor says. "I used to deliver really heavy sewing machinery. I've seen the whole neighborhood change. The hardest thing is seeing businesses go under."

The previous day, in fact, Taylor had delivered his last package to *Fine Art* magazine, at 147 West 25th Street. The August 2005 issue just published would be its last. Most of the young staffers ended up crying on Taylor's shoulder. "It was sad; they were telling me they were going to miss me," Taylor says. "What can you do? They come and go."

The goal of any UPS driver is that each package be delivered as efficiently as possible, taking the minimum of time, and exacting as small a toll on the body as possible. Taylor has been hurt exactly once in his thirty years at UPS, a pulled muscle in his back. He didn't miss any work. "The key to not getting injured," Taylor says as he reaches out for another package, "is not to twist. You bend your knees when you lift and you don't twist when reaching further back into the truck."

Mid-morning, Taylor goes through the package car to make sure he hasn't missed any early delivery packages. During inspection Taylor finds a damaged box, which he patches up with tape. Technology hasn't eliminated mishaps with packages, of course. Packages can get lost. Packages can get damaged. But as CEO Mike Eskew recently said in an interview in Atlanta, computers can never match the will of a motivated person like Taylor: "People make mistakes when they take shortcuts or get tired or get bored, but I'd rather have that spark in their eyes."

Customers don't fail to notice that Taylor and his fellow drivers, all 100,000-plus, go about their rounds with that gleam in their eyes. In fact, it's hard to believe that for almost the first half-century of its existence, UPS did hardly any business-to-business deliveries, but grew only through its consolidated retail delivery business, bringing packages from department stores to people's homes. The UPS of today, serving thousands of big and small businesses in all different industries, only emerged after a transformation sparked by fundamental socio-economic trends—shifts that would sideline not only other UPS competitors, but entire industries, for good.

A SEISMIC CHANGE IN THE MARKET

By mid-century, UPS had built a consolidated retail delivery business in metropolitan markets across the United States, one that generated decades of growth at the company.

Unfortunately, it was all about to fall apart.

First, with the outbreak of World War II and the imposition of wartime rationing, UPS's retail customers sharply curtailed deliveries. The federal government, through the Office of Price Administration, even encouraged "Carry Your Own Package" campaigns designed to conserve gasoline and tires. UPS swallowed hard and found what new business it could, hunkering down with deliveries for mail order giants like Sears and Montgomery Ward. Still, during the war years, UPS lost well over one-half of its total volume.

Prospects brightened with the return of peace in 1945, which unleashed a surge in consumer spending. But business at UPS did not fully revive, as department stores started to push back on the cost of deliveries and post-war inflation drove up the cost of business.

Internal cost-cutting measures made up some ground, as did a redoubled search for new customers to prop up volume. The company took on more furniture deliveries for department stores; expanded to Detroit, Minneapolis, and Pittsburgh; and managed to attract several large new customers in existing markets, including Macy's in 1946, which for the previous eighty-eight years of its existence had always made its own deliveries.

The long-term trend, however, was troubling. Measured by individual store, UPS's package volume kept falling. In 1941, UPS delivered ninety million pieces for customers. Ten years later, those same customers provided just seventy million deliveries. Total UPS volume was higher in 1951 than 1941 because of new customers, but the downward slope was inescapable. But the real problem wasn't post-World War II inflation or an inflexible UPS cost structure. Worse yet, there was nothing UPS could do about the real issue: The age of the automobile was overtaking the United States and UPS.

SUBURBS, CARS, AND PARKING LOTS: AN UNFORTUNATE COMBINATION FOR UPS

Between 1945 and 1955, the number of private automobiles registered in the United States doubled, from twenty-five million to fifty million. Then it nearly doubled again the ensuing decade. By 1960, more than four-fifths of American families owned at least one car. Cars carry people, but cars carry merchandise as well.

Suburbs inevitably followed pervasive car ownership. So, too, did supermarkets and shopping centers, new kinds of stores located on city outskirts that rapidly reshaped Americans patterns of buying and selling. These new grocery and department stores were typically very big and surrounded by spacious parking areas. Parking lots hadn't made much sense in urban settings, where relatively few customers had cars anyway.

But in this post-war, suburban landscape, they were becoming essential components of retailing, enabling customers to comfortably take their cars to stores from relatively long distances away. Unfortunately for UPS, the combination of automobile ownership, suburban stores, and parking lots made their service a lot less relevant.

Even more ominously, UPS's core customers, the major department stores, were joining the migration out of the cities. In the early 1950s, J.L. Hudson in Detroit, the May Company in Southern California, and Marshall Field's in Chicago were all building mammoth new facilities with parking lots for thousands of cars. It didn't take a genius to deduce that the end of the downtown department store era would also result in thousands of fewer deliveries for UPS.

RECOGNIZING A MOMENT OF TRUTH

UPS now faced a moment of truth. It could adopt a new business model, or it could stay the course, stagnating and hoping for the best.

But stagnation was unacceptable to the company's leaders. "A business that does not grow has little to offer employees, stockholders or customers," declared George Smith in 1953. Smith would go on to become UPS's second CEO in 1962. The real question wasn't whether to develop a new business model, but what this model would be.

There were several possibilities. Mail order deliveries and increased furniture deliveries offered some prospects, albeit limited ones. Air freight also looked potentially promising. But the most intriguing opportunity was wholesale deliveries. Having spent decades mastering consolidated delivery, UPS pretty much confined itself to carrying commerce out of retail businesses to consumers. Wholesale deliveries meant bringing goods *into* those stores from other businesses.

One advantage of this idea was that, with the advent of the car, highways—recognizably modern, multilane expressways complete with fast-food restaurants popping up every few miles—were being threaded across the continent, starting with the Maine Turnpike in 1947. A highway corridor between New York City and Chicago was completed in the late-1950s, and the Interstate Highway Act of 1956 created a blueprint for an even further developed system.

As this new infrastructure took shape, long-haul trucking emerged as a viable alternative to railroad freight. Rigs were built to carry twenty tons and more. Tractor-trailers, relatively rare before 1950, became commonplace, with more than a million driving the highways by 1960. Between 1950 and 1960, the volume of intercity freight carried by truck grew from 173 billion ton-miles to almost 300 billion, while railroad freight traffic fell from 597 billion ton-miles to 579 billion. In the 1960s, freight train volume would continue to fall.

UPS was already engaged in the wholesale business on a small scale on the West Coast. When it had entered Los Angeles, the company inherited a wholesale business that delivered from local wholesalers to local retailers. But wholesale business on any large scale offered intimidating barriers of entry.

First, due to various federal and state restrictions governing interstate commerce, a delivery company couldn't even bring deliveries from most states to another state, with a few exceptions. Needless to say, if UPS started fighting for the right to this business, plenty of entrenched trucking and railroad freight companies within each state stood ready to defend their territory. Second, UPS would be cultivating a much different base of customers, and carrying much denser, multidirectional kinds of commerce. Casey took pains to break it down in familiar terms for managers. They knew retail out-flows; now they would have to learn about retail in-flows. Third, in 1913 the U.S. Post Office inaugurated a parcel post service, meaning that the U.S. government would be competing directly with UPS.

By the early 1950s, however, the decay of the consolidated retail delivery business forced the company's hand. In what seemed like another sign, the U.S. Post Office stopped accepting parcels over twenty pounds early in 1952. In 1953, UPS experimented on a small scale by launching wholesale services in several pilot locations where traffic was busy and regulation relatively open. Also in 1953, in California, UPS received authorization to extend its reach into the wholesale trade in San Francisco and Oakland, and to connect its Los Angeles and San Francisco markets with wholesale service.

Long-haul carriers tried to block the move, but UPS placated opposition by demonstrating that the small volume it wanted was exactly that which the freight companies preferred to avoid. In San Francisco, UPS sales professionals began making cold calls to generate business and found a healthy market, with wholesale volume quickly reaching ten thousand packages a day.

The following year, the company began to build up wholesale business in Chicago's hinterland, starting with "a nucleus of about fifty small customers." Coverage was extended to 200 miles from the center of Chicago to counter competition from smaller, mom-and-pop delivery services. This move, along with tweaks in the rate schedule, brought in enough new customers to get business up to speed. In less than a year, UPS was already handling over 400 accounts and a daily volume of 5,000 packages in Chicago.

On June 4, 1954, UPS broke ground on a five-story, full block sorting hub southwest of the Chicago Loop, more proof that the company had turned the corner just a year into the wholesale experiment. A *Chicago Tribune* article about the project mentioned that the company had 600 wholesale accounts at the time. Also in 1954, George Smith could report that the new business "has come up to our expectations," and that the company was only "scratching the surface."

Naturally, early wholesale coverage tended to dovetail with areas where UPS served retail customers. In the suburbs, the company commingled retail deliveries with wholesale pickups, but in cities it initially handled the new business with a separate set of vehicles and routes. Either way, UPS drivers retained the brown uniforms and professional demeanor. UPS, as it turned out, still had a vital role to play in the delivery business.

SHIFTING STRATEGIC BEARINGS

As promising as the early wholesale business looked, it took some time for the company to realign itself strategically. Initially, Casey and Smith described the wholesale business as an ancillary venture, stressing the benefits it offered to the company's traditional core business. "One important reason for going into the wholesale field," the company argued in 1953, "is that the increased volume of small packages from that source should enable us to hold the cost per unit of retail deliveries to a lower point than would otherwise be possible."

In its annual report, the company at this stage was stressing the benefits that the new business would provide its traditional business. The expanding wholesale business would prop up UPS's sagging retail delivery business by lowering unit costs, extending service areas, and leveling out peak periods, such as the Christmas holidays.

The opportunities were constantly played down, and with good reason. Casey and Smith didn't want to raise the ire or interest of regulators, and likely didn't want competitors to realize the enormous demand that UPS was starting to find. Because the truth was that if UPS could overcome the regulatory hurdles, the prospects could make a less conservative company giddy. Wholesale delivery volume was growing rapidly, and doing so despite being confined to relatively narrow corridors of the company's operations. After all, if the company were free to pick up and deliver anywhere it chose, gaining small package business from the Parcel Post, the growth potential was enormous.

By 1956, wholesale business was beginning to supplant retail deliveries at the center of the company's thinking. Noting that retail delivery volume continued to slide while wholesale continued to surge, Casey decided it was time to put the situation in unambiguous terms. While noting in that year's annual report that the delivery of merchandise for retail stores was still the company's main business, he didn't shy away from the fact that UPS was shifting course: "The truth is that if we had to rely solely upon retail packages, the outlook for our company would not seem bright," he wrote.

ARTICULATING THE VISION AND EXECUTING CHANGE

A critical step in turning UPS into a wholesale business was communicating the new strategy to employees. Casey had to ensure that the sagging morale that had accompanied the mid-1950s deterioration of its core business didn't debilitate the new effort.

Without a modern "change management" text to guide him, Casey instinctively managed UPS through the greatest period of change. First, he acknowledged in the 1954 annual report that the company faced "a dismal outlook" if management did not have another vision for the company. Then, he described the vision: economic trends were creating the possibility of carrying commerce across much bigger spans of geography via modern highways and airplanes of increasing carrying capacity. The business of UPS would be nothing less than facilitating the commerce of the continent. Finally, he laid out a time frame to achieve the change, saying that in ten years UPS should, in addition to continuing serving retail stores, be delivering wholesale small packages by automobile or airplane, to any city or town in the United

States within two days. If all went right, UPS would be handling millions of packages going into businesses of all kinds.

The proposal was audacious. A road-based, truck and package-car carried network had never been built on a national scale by a commercial company before. In fact, what UPS was preparing to undertake was analogous to the forging of the national rail and telegraph networks in the nineteenth century.

To pull it off, UPS was going to have to get much bigger. The larger the territory that UPS had a presence in, the more packages it could pick up. Too, unlike the consolidated retail delivery business, which took shape on the ground as a series of essentially unconnected local operations, the new business would have to be tightly interconnected.

Casey was also concerned about the cultural impact of a new UPS. To this point, UPS's structure had enabled managers and employees to foster a tangible sense of local ownership, both literally and figuratively. In day-to-day terms, the business of department store delivery was a profoundly local one.

Now that UPS faced the challenge of growing out to unprecedented dimensions, it could not afford to lose the initiative, the energy and commitment that had already proven such potent ingredients in the company's culture. To that end, the bedrock values of promote-from-within, employee ownership, and drivers devoted to service and integrity were continually reinforced.

In a remarkable talk to company leadership in 1956, Casey delivered a change management message that was addressed to no one—and to everyone. Famous inside UPS, "A Talk with

Joe" hinted at the company's business model which centered on everyman "Joe":

> In the world of business, favorable opportunities are where you find them. The prizes go to those who are ready. New industries, new kinds of business, are particularly promising to people who get into them early, because there is the chance to share in their growth. You and I, Joe, are fortunate to be in what is really a new business, notwithstanding the company's half-century of existence.

FROM WHOLESALE TO COMMON CARRIER

Casey set a goal of achieving comprehensive coverage of the United States with wholesale delivery within ten years. In fact, it took UPS more than three decades to achieve this milestone. What started in 1952 as an effort to add wholesale traffic became a campaign to forge what UPS began calling the Golden Link, meaning contiguous states through which UPS could deliver packages from one coast to the other.

Obtaining regulatory authority took concerted effort all along the way, consuming substantial time and energy, region by region, state by state, regulatory hearing by regulatory hearing. Numerous entrenched interests, from long-haul freight companies like Railway Express to bus companies and small package delivery companies, tried to block UPS from entering new territories, marshalling what former UPS CEO Oz Nelson describes as "a whole raft of lawyers" each time. But UPS was no slouch in the legal arena, with in-house attorneys like Joe Tranfo, who recruited thousands of witnesses from small businesses to testify that UPS offered a much-needed service, to Philadelphia attorneys Bernie and Buddy Segal, "demanding, brazen men" according to Nelson, but incredibly competent as well.

There were some casualties of the laser-like focus on forging the Golden Link. As one example, the company launched an air express service in 1953, more than two decades after the United Air Express experiment had failed. Eventually known as Blue Label Air, the air service offered two-day service between certain major cities in various parts of the country. But more attention might have been paid to the potential of an air express service using the hub-and-spoke model that UPS had perfected on the ground.

In 1975, the company reached a milestone when it inaugurated overland service between the West Coast and Eastern and Midwestern states, formally forging the Golden Link.

Coverage became comprehensive in 1980 when the Federal Interstate Commerce Commission removed a 100-pound weight limit on shipments from one customer to one address, and authorized UPS to serve retailers on an interstate basis in common carrier operations throughout the United States. Through twenty-eight years of slow building, UPS had transformed itself from a retail deliverer operating in scattered metropolitan markets into a common carrier capable of picking up and delivering packages anywhere in the United States.

Some of the battles were particularly bruising; for example, it took UPS three attempts and more than two decades before eventually triumphing over Texas's railroad commission and winning the right to provide intrastate deliveries in Texas in 1986.

For UPS, large-scale, corporate-wide change did not spring from the omniscient inspiration of a strategic visionary, issue forth at the charismatic command of a heroic leader, or dramatically sweep the company into a new field of business. UPS achieved transformation by working slowly and methodically, from the inside out. In this respect, the common carrier story is a classic UPS narrative.

And while the changeover to becoming a common carrier was arduous, the willingness to transform was clearly embedded in the company's DNA. In the coming years, transformations would come more quickly, and more dramatically, as business conditions changed.

UPS RULES FOR THE ROAD

A Common and Uncommon Carrier:
Accomplishing Transformation

- **Create your own luck.** Film director Samuel Goldwyn once said, "The harder I work, the luckier I get." UPS did not wait until the complete demise of its retail business model before setting its sights on a new direction serving wholesale customers. Don't be a victim of situations—create your own situations.

- **Help employees understand the company's "narrative."** Changing the behavior of even one person can be a challenge. Persuading hundreds or thousands of employees is something else altogether. Managers need to educate employees on where the company is heading—and what's in it for them—in order to achieve fundamental organizational change.

- **Express empathy toward employees.** Empathy won't be found anywhere in an annual report, but by adopting this aspect of UPS management, companies can increase retention rates and loyalty when they undergo major transformation.

4

Rising to the FedEx Challenge:
Building an Airline

"The well-run companies have a bias for action."

—George Lamb,

UPS CEO, 1980–1984

WHEN TRADE TRUMPED INTERNATIONAL TENSIONS

On April 1, 2001, UPS launched its maiden voyage from the United States directly into China, a flight that UPS had lobbied for as hard as it had ever fought for anything. As it turned out, the timing couldn't have been worse. The Boeing 747 was en route from Anchorage to Shanghai when a breaking story reached the crew.

A U.S. Navy reconnaissance plane had collided with a Chinese F-8 fighter jet over international waters off the coast of China. The Chinese pilot was missing and presumed dead, and damage to the U.S. plane forced the Americans to land on the Chinese island of Hainan. Denouncing the surveillance mission as an encroachment on national sovereignty, Chinese authorities seized the U.S. crew and the plane, over strong U.S. objections.

Diplomats on both sides of the Pacific Ocean scrambled to contain the spreading crisis.

UPS, tempted to turn its plane around and wait for calmer skies, decided that it had done too much work to turn back. The company had been struggling to extend its global network into China, which meant gaining landing rights at Chinese airports. Tightly controlled by the Chinese government, these rights had been issued to just three U.S. carriers up until 1999: Northwest, United, and Flying Tigers, which was purchased by FedEx in 1989.

That year, after extensive lobbying by the United States, China agreed to grant landing rights to a fourth U.S. airline. One of the fiercest aviation route applications in history ensued, with the U.S. Department of Transportation presiding. Many passenger airlines vied for the prize, and FedEx, hoping to preserve its cargo monopoly, leant political support. UPS itself mobilized a massive lobbying campaign behind the principle of "trade, not tourists." In 1999 UPS was awarded the flights.

The opening came at a crucial juncture for the company. UPS was aggressively expanding its global network and recasting itself as something bigger than just a domestic U.S. package company. What better way to demonstrate this newfound modernity than by flying new routes into the world's biggest market?

UPS arranged gala commemorative ceremonies at Newark, where the Browntail took off, and Ontario, California, where it stopped en route to Anchorage, as well as in Beijing. UPS executives, delegates from the Teamsters and other unions, DOT officials, and other dignitaries gathered to mark the occasion and toast the flight.

Now, with its first flight into China just hours from touching down in Shanghai and with the U.S. and Chinese government exchanging rhetoric, UPS and the crew decided that they should go ahead and do the job. What had begun as a public relations triumph was instead becoming a frightening mission.

But when the Browntail descended into Shanghai, it was met with a reception just as warm as its send-off. Chinese authorities, as it turned out, had no intention of letting geopolitics mar a significant milestone in China's entry into the global marketplace. The UPS crew was warmly welcomed not only by politicians and business executives, but also by several hundred Chinese schoolchildren singing their own greeting. Commerce had trumped national rivalry, and UPS had carried the company's scope of operation into yet another frontier of commerce.

THE TROUBLE WITH SUCCESS

UPS is defined in the popular imagination by its drivers and brown package cars. But it also runs the eighth-largest airline in the world, serving more than 800 airports in more than 200 countries and territories around the world. Right now, in fact— 24-hours-a-day, 365-days-a-year—UPS planes are in the sky.

UPS Airlines employs some 1,200 captains and another 1,500 first officers and second officers, as well as 1,200 mechanics. The company owns and operates almost 300 Browntails and charters hundreds more aircraft.

By the time it committed to building this airline, UPS had been in business for more than seventy-five years and had forged world-class ground operations. Yet it had also grown complacent, and its intense corporate culture of industrial engineering and operations excellence was, in some ways, about to become an obstacle. Like so many companies, UPS was going to have to unlearn some of the very traits that had made it so successful.

GETTING BACK INTO THE AIR BUSINESS

Strictly speaking, UPS started building its airline in the early 1980s, when the company bought its first jets. But Casey always liked to point out that the Wright Brothers made their historic flights only a few years before UPS was created. The events at Kitty Hawk definitely gripped the founder's imagination, and he and his partners were soon looking for ways to harness the technology and the opportunities it created. The company started an air service called United Air Express. It failed, and it was more than twenty years later before the company tried again.

That was in 1953, when the company ushered in United Parcel Service-Air, inaugurating shipments between large U.S. cities like Los Angeles, San Francisco, New York, Philadelphia, Chicago, and Detroit. Undertaken as the company's core consolidated retail delivery business deteriorated, the business consisted of UPS leasing space on airlines. But the venture did put UPS back in the air express business, "express" in this case defined as two-day transit.

Rechristened "Blue Label" in 1967, the air business remained small and, strategically speaking, something of a sideline. From the 1950s through the 1970s, UPS remained preoccupied with building out a comprehensive ground delivery network capable of picking up and delivering packages anywhere in the United States. Still, the company did manage to expand the scope of Blue Label coverage in successive stages. By 1977, UPS's air shipment service blanketed the United States.

In 1978, deregulation removed restrictions obstructing the movement of airfreight. The conditions had fallen in place for building a new breed of hybrid ground-air network. But UPS would not be the first company to figure out how to harness the opportunity.

THE FEDEX CHALLENGE

Unlike its common carrier business, UPS's Blue Label air service contended with experienced and effective competitors. By the late 1970s, Emery, Airborne, and Purolator were all jockeying Blue Label for elbow room in the skies. The sharpest elbows, though, belonged to a hungry new company that burst onto the scene in 1972 with an innovative business model that would ultimately redefine the airfreight industry, encroach on UPS's core businesses, and force UPS to rethink fundamental strategic assumptions.

Federal Express first took shape as an idea hatched by founder Fred Smith as a Yale undergraduate. While writing a term paper about shipping by plane versus shipping by truck, Smith came to believe that the routes forged by the airline industry were not only accidental and random in nature, but wholly ineffective. Smith's argument was, essentially, as long as airplanes focused on the movement of people, they could never move time-sensitive, high-value items quickly, as a hub-and-spoke delivery model would.

Despite the fact that UPS had perfected a ground-based hub-and-spoke system years earlier, the company apparently never saw the viability of this approach applied to an air network.

Also observing that most airfreight shippers, UPS included, piggy-backed on inefficient passenger route systems, Smith decided to set up a company structured specifically to provide expedited shipping, on a premium basis, for time-sensitive, small packages such as legal documents, medical supplies, computer parts, and electronics. With money from a family trust fund, Smith incorporated and in April 1973, Federal Express made its first deliveries, ferrying 186 packages in fourteen Dassault Falcon jets to twenty-five U.S. destinations.

The company's hub-and-spoke system, with Memphis as the sorting hub, created the most efficient next day air operation in the industry. FedEx still took three years to turn a profit as it invested heavily to build out its infrastructure, and then it needed several more years of lobbying to break down regulatory barriers preventing the use of larger aircraft.

But Smith's energy and entrepreneurial savvy attracted an aggressive, resourceful team of managers and ushered in a string of innovations. New technologies and products pioneered by FedEx included a centralized computer system to track packages in 1979, the Digitally Assisted Dispatch System (DADS) that coordinated customers' on-call pickups in 1980, and the Overnight Letter in 1981.

By the early 1980s, FedEx had revolutionized the airfreight business and established itself as the leading overnight delivery provider. What UPS had done for ground-based consolidated delivery systems in the 1920s and 1930s, FedEx did for next day air operations in the 1970s and early 1980s.

All of which UPS watched with some concern, but, at first, not with any real sense of urgency. After all, FedEx did not put itself in direct competition with UPS's ground dominance, but instead focused early efforts on building its own premium overnight business.

The surprise for UPS came when the size of the market that FedEx had tapped into started to become clear. Particularly at law firms, financial concerns, investment houses, and other such purveyors of important, timely information, the enthusiasm was overwhelming for a service that could guarantee delivery of that information the next day.

FedEx took advantage of this market by making a strong impression on customers. The upstart offered on-call pickups, for example, something UPS had never done in the U.S. As it honed its operational capability, FedEx began promising delivery not just by the next day, but by 10:30 a.m. the next day.

High-profile advertising in the national media, meanwhile, captured the popular imagination, helping to make "FedEx" not just an abbreviation for a hot new company, but a verb as well. UPS's Blue Label, by contrast, which offered two-day service for 70 percent less than FedEx's overnight delivery price, made do with much more modest advertising, because UPS felt that the UPS brand was so well known.

By the early 1980s, customers were beginning to ask UPS drivers and sales professionals why UPS wasn't offering next day delivery. UPS, a company that had built its reputation and name on the high standards of its service, had been outplayed at its own game. Its methodical and tightly controlled systems had created a powerfully effective ground network, but also inflexible service from some customers' point of view. When customers asked if UPS could provide discounts to its larger customers, or if it could stop by a little later or earlier in the day, they were told that that's not how UPS did things.

UPS got the message quickly enough. As Tom Weidemeyer, former UPS COO who led UPS Airlines in the 1990s, puts it: "We discovered that we'd better wake up. Customers clearly wanted international shipping, package tracking, and overnight service."

First, UPS was going to have to dramatically augment its air capability. The company could try expanding and adapting its Blue Label network, which was still flying packages by charter freighters. That option looked dubious, particularly if UPS wanted to make an overnight service work. The alternative of assembling and operating a UPS fleet was daunting, though. The airline business was highly complex, heavily regulated, and entirely unfamiliar.

Looking for a middle road, UPS decided in 1981 to buy airplanes, but rely on a group of four independent carriers to handle the operations. Officially, that meant that UPS wasn't an airline and wouldn't be regulated by the FAA. After purchasing nine used Boeing 727–100s, UPS needed to find people in the organization who knew something about the business.

"Back then, we knew zero about airplanes," remembers retired UPS employee Patrick O'Leary. Like almost everyone else in the company, O'Leary was a "ground guy," starting as a part-time supervisor while attending college and then working his way up the management ranks. Thanks to a stint in the Marine Corps, though, O'Leary had acquired experience as a helicopter pilot. This credential was enough to move him to the air side of the business in January 1982, and it was painfully clear to O'Leary how little anyone at UPS knew about the business. He recalled hearing one time when a pilot called in reporting that the plane had tumbled a gyro. "Is that bad?" O'Leary remembers a colleague asking. "Well, yeah," he responded. "That means the plane's navigation system isn't functioning."

UPS debuted overnight service in August 1982 between West Coast cities, that classic proving ground that had launched both UPS's common carrier service and United Parcel Service-Air. The planes were even painted with UPS brown, thus the term *Browntails.*

Expectations ran high in September 1982 as the company prepared its nationwide launch of Next Day Air, serving twenty-four cities. UPS Air team members traveled to Louisville for a ceremony commemorating the milestone. Expectantly, the visitors watched as the first plane landed—with only 150 packages. Those gathered had been guessing the total volume for the first day for all twenty-four cities, and no one had guessed below 10,000 packages. They were way off: UPS Air delivered 1,800 packages that day, a number that was rather humiliating. The company realized that the UPS brand didn't attract air volume the way it attracted ground volume.

"We thought the carriers would take care of everything for us, because we had no expertise," relates Dick Oehme, who, as head of UPS air operations, was in charge of coordinating with the carriers.

But UPS persevered, stepping up marketing efforts. Coverage, along with the size of the fleet, expanded in several phases over the next year. By 1985, UPS was offering Next Day Air across the continental United States and preparing to launch its air service to European destinations.

As volume began to grow, the business grew increasingly awkward to operate at arm's length. Operating under the carriers' four certificates, the UPS fleet had four separate sets of flight operations, four maintenance schedules, and four groups of pilots affiliated with the different carriers. In addition, UPS could not interchange planes among the carriers. So, for example, if one plane was grounded waiting for a part, resting adjacent to a fully operational plane certified under another carrier, the crew from the first plane could not fly the second plane. "A lot of those kinds of issues emerged as the business got larger," Oehme says. "The talk had always been, 'We will not be an airline.' But volume was growing, and we needed to have control."

The inherent limits of the strategy repeatedly left UPS hamstrung. In 1987, one of UPS's carriers, Orion, ran into certification problems with the FAA, which promptly grounded the airline until the issue could be resolved. All of a sudden, UPS was down thirteen airplanes. The company scraped together enough spare aircraft from its other carriers, supplemented by a hastily mustered fleet of smaller, leased jets to plug the gaps. It was clearly time for UPS to rethink the entire approach and consider becoming an airline.

The process was fraught with risk. First, it would require a massive commitment of resources and money; second, airline labor norms were completely unfamiliar to UPS; and third, UPS knew very little about operating an airline.

But Oehme and Mike Eskew, then head of engineering for UPS Air, went before the Board of Directors and explained that UPS could not maintain service and grow as a company by operating through the independent carriers. Subsequently, in August 1987, UPS announced it would take control of its fleet and maintenance operations and apply to become an official airline. It wasn't long before UPS heard from FAA officials. The agency warned UPS that it was attempting to assemble the most ambitious start-up certification in the history of U.S. aviation. UPS had its work cut out.

CREATING AN AIRLINE IN ONE YEAR OR LESS

The challenges were apparent enough that UPS understood that even a top-notch team of ground operations managers were going to need help from folks who knew the air business. In the next few months, UPS would hire more people, faster, from outside UPS than ever before, a pace that would only be rivaled by the company's ramp-up in technology a few years later. The airline industry hires were often retired or semi-retired, old pros who knew what hazards UPS faced and could help the company steer clear.

They were paired, one-to-one, with UPS veterans with a bent toward learning a different side of the business. The airline pros learned about UPS and vice versa. Warren Johnson, UPS director of airline maintenance, says that, "The key to making the whole thing work was mixing airline outsiders with brown-blooders."

The strategy team met every Friday to review progress function by function, making sure everything was going as planned. Applying for FAA certification as an airline required a mountain of paperwork. Johnson had already been involved in two other start-ups, both much smaller in scale than UPS, and each of which took the better part of a year to get off the ground. UPS was working in an even shorter time frame and trying to become qualified as a much bigger airline. The job was even more intimidating in that UPS had to contend with the complexity of merging four carrier certifications, even as it underwent its own certification, and keep its operation running every day.

CULTURAL TENSIONS

UPS had to hire pilots, of course, no less than 800 to get the airline off the ground. For a company as fiercely protective of its culture as UPS, the hiring process turned out to be a difficult, often contentious series of adaptations and adjustments. UPS had to figure out how to integrate, at once, a huge number of professionals used to being the most important people in their organization. "We ran into a bit of turbulence at first," concedes Rick Barr, vice president of UPS's airline operations.

Actually, "a bit of turbulence" would be a serious understatement.

UPS had much to learn about pilots. UPS managers had spent much of their careers in package cars and sorting centers, and the world of the airline pilot was a different one. Pilots identified strongly with their profession, and it took time for everyone to get on the same page culturally. As a small example, pilots wanted to be addressed by other UPS employees as "Captain," even though the CEO and other top managers of the company went by first names like everyone else.

Another issue was the typical airline industry definition of "late." UPS, of course, measured everything to the second because of the nature of its business. By the FAA's definition, however, a flight wasn't even considered late until it reached a delay of fourteen minutes, which is at least thirteen minutes more than UPS can spare.

"As far as [passenger] airlines are concerned, it's not really a big deal to be, say, fifteen minutes late. But UPS doesn't accept anything but perfect service," says Weidemeyer. As Weidemeyer points out, a 747 full of packages an hour late that misses that night's sort leaves up to 30,000 people unhappy on the sending and receiving sides of the equation.

Both the pilots and UPS management had adjustments to make as the company absorbed the dynamics of air operations. Tensions ran particularly high at the gateways, where ground handlers and pilots handed volume off to one another. One incident in Alaska is indicative of the types of misunderstandings that were common. Entering a landing approach and encountering a thick bank of fog, a UPS pilot pulled out of the landing.

When the Browntail made the landing on a second approach and pulled into the gate, an infuriated gateway supervisor demanded to know why the pilot was pulling in twenty minutes late. Unbeknownst to the supervisor on the ground, the pilot had not pulled up because of the fog, but a regulatory designation that restricted the altitude at which the plane could make its approach.

UPS's gateway staff eventually had to accept the reality that they had far less control over air operations than ground operations. For example, if an airline mechanic doing a pre-flight checklist decided that the de-icing job was not good enough, it would have to be redone, according to FAA regulations. The delay might give the gateway manager fits, but the judgment of the mechanic must be taken seriously when it comes to air travel. It all adds up to UPS consistently having the best safety record of any U.S. airline.

FINDING MIDDLE GROUND

UPS Air and the ground operation eventually did cultivate a patch of middle ground. After all, pilots, as UPS pilot Shelley Pennington points out, are a very procedure-oriented breed; or as she puts it, "as far as we're concerned, there's a process to everything." Shadowing any crewmember through a pre-flight check drives the point home: these are professionals trained to approach their jobs as a series of interconnected, team-driven tasks and responsibilities, which sounds a good deal like UPS's approach to handling ground operations.

Today, through leadership workshops UPS started in the late 1990s, pilots meet with hub managers and sort supervisors, ride with drivers in package cars, and meet with district managers to discuss improving service at the company that they all work for.

The exposure is often revelatory for pilots typically disconnected from UPS drivers, the people closest to the customer. Says Pennington: "It's important that they meet the people who are the face of UPS, hearing everyone say 'hi' to the driver, and realizing what UPS is all about."

UPS RULES FOR THE ROAD

Rising to the FedEx Challenge:
Building an Airline

- **Team building is essential for organizational success.** When UPS became an airline in 1988, its new pilots had a slightly different attitude on the importance of their role in the company versus, say, that of the company's drivers. Exposure to other jobs at UPS helped the pilots understand that every job is important in creating a service environment, and that all employees are valued in their contribution to organizational success.

- **Get on board or get off the tracks.** While UPS may have been slow to jump into the overnight express business, once it decided to move, it created a nationwide network in just over a year. Likewise, when the company determined it needed to operate its own airline, it accomplished the fastest start-up in FAA history.

5

Beyond the Golden Link:
Going International

"Our purpose is to enable global commerce."

—JIM KELLY,

UPS CEO, 1997-2001

ONE CITY, TWO CONTINENTS

Each weekday afternoon amidst the mosques and minarets of Istanbul, Turkey—a city more than twice the area of the country of Luxembourg—UPS package cars traverse the Bosphorus Strait, that ancient dividing line between Europe and Asia that flows through the city center.

The odd fact of UPS simultaneously delivering packages within one city but between two continents is fitting for its operations in Istanbul, known as a commercial crossroads for millennia. Connecting the Black Sea to the Mediterranean, the Bosphorus has been a coveted trade route for silk, spices, and textiles for more than 2,000 years, controlled variously by the Roman, Byzantine, and Ottoman empires, as well as—more recently—Turkish military governments and the current republic alike.

For UPS, though, the Bosphorus is not an avenue of commerce but instead an obstacle to it: a twenty-mile-long, one-mile-wide conundrum that throws a wrench each night into UPS achieving its mission of getting packages on the nightly 9:10 P.M. flight from Istanbul to the company's European air hub in Cologne, Germany.

The sparkling, newly renovated Istanbul Ataturk Airport sits on the European side of the Bosphorus, meaning that companies such as UPS that are located on the Asian (or "Anatolian" side as Turks still refer to it), face a gauntlet of obstacles to make the 9:10 departure. Just two bridges span the Strait to link the bifurcated city (nineteen bridges connect the various boroughs of New York City, by contrast) and there is only one road to the airport in a metropolis that has tripled in population over the past two decades, to fifteen million people.

To reach that thoroughfare and brave all its congestion for any chance at getting to the airport on time, UPS drivers like Yusuf Yayuz and Senol Demircan must travel unpaved, circuitous alleys and streets on both sides of the Bosphorus. "You can't go on the main roads here," says Yayuz. "The traffic is too bad. You would never get anywhere." If it rains heavily, the back roads become thick with mud and what should be an hour trip can easily turn into three hours. Commercial construction projects also clog many UPS routes, and UPS drivers are always dodging the cars and small trucks parked haphazardly all over narrow, cobble-stoned trading warrens in the manufacturing districts of Istanbul. "We call leaving your vehicle anywhere you want 'parking Turkish,'" says Engin Sarioglu, the thirty-year-old manager of UPS in the main Istanbul package sorting center.

Parking Turkish doesn't cause any real problems when one moves as fast and efficiently as Demircan, a thirty-year-old driver who has been working for UPS in Turkey for nine years. Demircan will do about eighty stops today, most of them at Turkish textile companies eager to get their goods on that evening flight. Because he has a van and not a package car (Istanbul limits how much cargo can be carried into and out of the city limits), Demircan must return to the package sorting center several times, unload, and go back on the route again.

Demircan's shuttling to and from the sorting center is all the more impressive given the 6,500-square-kilometer size of Istanbul. The city is so sprawling that UPS has divided it into 180 different delivery routes and devised its own coding system to catalogue them, since Turkish postal codes, similar to those in Japan, China, and Korea, generally just confuse matters. "There are postal codes for Istanbul, but they are not exactly logical," is how Sarioglu bluntly describes the situation.

Postal codes or no, missing the 9:10 P.M. flight means another twenty-four hours before an express package can leave Turkey. There is no UPS ground network between Turkey and the eight countries bordering it. A package going from Istanbul bound for Greece, just over the border, must first get flown west to the Cologne air hub and then back east to Greece. "There are kinks in the system, but that's the way it works in Turkey," Sarioglu says, "and for UPS in Turkey it has worked very well."

True enough. A custom-made suit can be ordered from London, custom-tailored in Istanbul that day, put on the 9:10, and reach London via UPS by the time the shop opens the next morning.

THE TURKISH MARKET: THE PERFECT UPS CUSTOMERS?

The economic principles governing UPS's international air business are straightforward enough. The costs of capital-intensive package sorting centers, vans, feeder trucks, and airplanes are basically fixed, so the idea is to maximize the two variables that really push up profit margins on international deliveries: package weight and, especially, speed of delivery.

Putting as much express volume on intercontinental flights as possible, as opposed to second- or third-day deliveries—or just cargo—is still one of the biggest challenges facing UPS today. The problem is particularly acute on planes moving from the United States to China and Southeast Asia, as the U.S. trade deficit with those parts of the world is reflected in the less-than-full UPS planes on those routes. "Our perfect international customer would send heavy packages that need to arrive in a hurry, and those packages would not be overly discounted," says David Abney, UPS chief operating officer and former president of its International division.

Judged on Abney's categorization of what makes a superior international air express customer, UPS customers in Turkey appear to be ideal. Turkish companies send largely bulk shipments like textiles and automotive parts; the packages are typically sent express because customers are anxiously awaiting arrival on the other end; and most Turkish companies don't give UPS enough volume to qualify for deep discounts. On his route, for example, Demircan picks up from several customers in the Istanbul leather textile district leather jackets and full-length coats that have been ordered in Paris and London and need to reach their destinations by the next day.

When one brings up outsourcing today, everyone naturally thinks of China. China is certainly the place for producing a wide range of manufactured goods, and India and Uzbekistan are perfect for turning out thousands of white T-shirts (a surfeit of cotton being available in those two locales). But London or Milan retailers hoping to sell high-end suits at $2,000 a pop and $300 designer jeans still rely on both Turkish tailoring and styling. "Labor is cheaper here than in Europe, and we have the experience and technology to do very high-quality textiles," says Haluk Undeger, an agent for UPS in Turkey.

Chinese manufacturers, for example, typically can't do the high-end embroidery or graphics that go on designer T-shirts (though it's probably just a matter of time before they do so, and then subcontract out much of the low-skill work currently done there to countries like Laos and Cambodia.) Small and mid-sized Turkish textile companies, on the other hand, specialize in designing and manufacturing seven or eight different samples of high fashion T-shirts for well-known brands. "Our customers need samples for their big retail customers, and might want five T-shirt designs in five different colors to test at a big meeting," says Tolga Binga, UPS Turkey's director of marketing.

The 9:10 P.M. flight gets these Turkish T-shirt samples, suits, leather jackets, and carpets into Cologne around midnight. From Cologne, thirty-five or so planes take off every morning between 1 A.M. and 4 A.M., bringing the Turkish-manufactured goods to carpet dealers in America, department stores in Italy, and suit retailers in London.

THE UPS STORY IN ISTANBUL

UPS provides service in Turkey through a local agent relationship, rather than by employing its own personnel. Of the more than 220 countries and territories served by UPS, about 10 percent of the volume is served through agents and joint ventures.

Haluk Undeger is one of UPS's most successful agents. A vibrant, bushy-haired forty-six-year-old multimillionaire, he runs a company called Unsped, of which UPS Turkey is one division. In its agent relationships, UPS actually doesn't own the businesses; the agent simply offers UPS-branded service under its own umbrella and is compensated for these services. Of course, UPS has controls and standards in place to ensure compliance with service levels and other aspects of the operation.

Unsped actually competes with UPS in Turkey because it offers both its own package delivery service within Istanbul, as well as large-scale logistics solutions, akin to UPS Supply Chain Solutions. Does UPS management mind competing with Undeger's other Unsped businesses? CEO Eskew responds: "The great thing about Turkey is that it shows we can achieve results without having to own the business, that there is room to do things differently around the world."

Indeed, things are done differently at UPS Turkey. Call center operators pick up same-day delivery calls from tiny businesses and individual customers. There is no automated pre-load; actually there is no pre-load at all. Inside the package sorting center Demircan and his fellow drivers stand by the blue conveyor—where Istanbul-bound packages are routed—spy an address from their route, pick it up, and put it in neatly stacked piles next to their vans. These UPS drivers don't use the DIAD either, but instead a hand-held computer developed especially by UPS Turkey engineers.

But UPS has managed to export to Turkey both the UPS culture and many of its processes. "If you look at an operation like Turkey, or those in many other parts of the world, they haven't yet used technology to automate everything, but they still use the same UPS processes," says UPS CIO Dave Barnes. "They scan, customers can track packages, they have a set product portfolio, and the drivers are top-notch."

Chain-smoking Marlboros and drinking tiny cups of Turkish tea one after the other, Undeger led a visitor one day in the summer of 2006 on a tour of the Unsped and UPS operations. Not only does Undeger's UPS service offer brown vehicles and uniformed drivers, but Undeger is no doubt one of UPS's biggest cheerleaders between Atlanta and Shanghai.

To wit: The counter of the UPS customer service center in the building lobby is actually a five-foot-long model of a Browntail. The primary school Undeger helped pay for is emblazoned with a giant UPS logo on an outside wall, visible from blocks away. Above one of the basketball rims in the school gym hangs another model Browntail. A rug in Undeger's office is embroidered with a scene of a UPS driver making his rounds. "UPS has taught me everything," Undeger likes to say. "They are the big brother here in Turkey, and Unsped is the little brother."

UPS AND UNSPED

As a young man, Undeger grew his small customs brokerage into a profitable business and was waiting in the wings when the big opportunity came. In 1987, the Turkish military government was overthrown and the whole of Turkey was opened for trade. Huge shipments were coming into and out of the country every day and Unsped was clearing customs for a large portion of it. The incredibly dynamic and fast-moving environment made Undeger a wealthy man, yes, but was also perfect training for a future UPS partner.

In 1988, as part of its larger plan to offer global service to its customers, UPS interviewed more than 100 Turkish couriers and customs brokers in the hopes of finding a good agent to help it expand business to Turkey, and picked Unsped after a long, eight-month process. On October 2, 1988, UPS started making the Istanbul-to-Cologne flight.

For a time, some Turkish customers didn't exactly understand how to send a package via UPS. In those first years UPS was housed in a mustard-colored building that today stands adjacent to the current UPS building. Undeger, even then obviously enthusiastic about model Browntails, erected a large model of a UPS plane on the roof of the building. More than once customers rushed up to the building and into the lobby saying they needed to get a package on that plane before it took off.

MAKING THE AIRPORT

Sarioglu, the operations manager, is the man in the middle of the action responsible for ensuring that UPS packages reach the airport on time. He coordinates the thirty-five or so vans and feeder trucks that operate out of this main hub. Several other small UPS package sorting centers are distributed throughout

Istanbul, and there are about 250 vehicles in the UPS Turkey network.

A trained engineer, Sarioglu is one of the few college graduates working down in the sort. He's been with UPS for six years and cut his teeth at the airport operation, where UPS combines this volume with about twice as much from the rest of greater Istanbul. At about 7:30 P.M. each day in early summer, ceramics, carpets, tapestries, and other goods are brought into the package center by Demircan, Yayuz, and about twenty other drivers to be consolidated onto a single feeder truck bound for the airport.

The most time-sensitive packages, though, will never reach this sort. UPS in Turkey has set up an innovative mobile sorting and processing unit near the airport. A UPS feeder truck with scanning capability awaits just outside the airport grounds so that customers can wait until the very, very last minute to rush their packages themselves to the truck, knowing that the cutoff time is a mere fifteen minutes before flight time. The unit has its own generator and Internet access so that package information can be uploaded into the UPS system.

Two UPS drivers work this mini-sort, scanning packages, printing out and affixing the labels, and, then, at about 9:05 P.M., speeding off to the airplane. "In Turkey, business is based on flexibility and unknowns, because traffic might be terrible or maybe something breaks and you need more time to get stuff done," Sarioglu says. "At UPS we are very flexible to give our customers the most time."

While it sounds unusual, this particular service is really just an offshoot of other UPS operations. For Undeger, it's another opportunity to do things a little differently. After all, UPS's successful recipe for international growth includes a healthy dose of letting locals run the business—especially when it is *their* business. "We don't want to be a U.S. company doing business in Turkey," says COO Abney. "We want to be a Turkish company in Turkey."

INITIAL SALLIES

In 1975, with the Golden Link finally completed under CEO Harold Oberkotter's leadership, UPS had the authority to link its service within the forty-eight contiguous states. Hawaii, thanks to a UPS acquisition, was also linked, and Alaska soon would be, meaning that UPS served all fifty states. But as former labor and public relations manager Joe Tranfo puts it, "UPS was built to expand; it was almost second-nature." And UPS certainly wasn't going to stop expanding because of a small matter like running out of states. It was time to take the business and duplicate it in an international market.

The thinking back then was that UPS's non-United States revenue opportunities were primarily intra-country. Trading patterns in the mid-1970s largely ran along well-trodden Cold War political fissures, and the globalization and cross-border commerce that blossomed in the 1990s was hardly hinted at by the geopolitical calculus of the day.

The question was which country offered the best intra-country market?

In 1972, eighty-four-year-old Jim Casey had taken it upon himself to travel to West Germany and investigate the market for expansion. He spent most of his time in the northern city of Hamburg, where the German post office, or *Bundespost*, kept its main parcel sorting center. Casey believed that West Germany with its booming economy made the perfect beachhead for UPS into Europe, especially compared to the strike-wracked U.K. and the French preoccupation with labor issues during that period.

But the time wasn't right, not with the Golden Link still incomplete. And not in early 1975, either. Oberkotter, instead, wanted to proceed cautiously and formed a small working group to investigate the idea of expanding to West Germany.

Besides, now that UPS served the entire United States, Canada seemed like the most logical and low-risk choice for expansion. There were virtually no cultural issues, few or no language issues (even in Quebec province, English was just as much the language of business as French), and Toronto was an easy trip for UPS executives. As a bonus, the ease of border crossings between the two countries meant that UPS could actually run its first import-export business and not limit its Canadian operations to just domestic Canadian service. On February 28, 1975—nearly sixty-eight years after the company started in Seattle—UPS began its Canadian service in Toronto, the company's first operation based outside of the United States.

Like Jim Casey's basement business in Seattle, UPS Canada started out below street level, with UPS Canada president Glenn Smith and his team renting out the basement office of a Toronto-area hotel called the Skyline. The first pickup was a good one: fifteen packages from the Butterick Fashions Marketing Company.

Almost right away it became clear that various constituencies within the Canadian government were not going to make things overly easy for UPS. First, UPS was denied the authority to operate commercial vehicles in Ontario and was forced to find something else in which to deliver packages. To replace tractor-trailer feeder trucks, UPS settled on Checker cabs, about twice as roomy as normal passenger cars. With their backseats removed and outfitted with roof racks and U-Haul trailers, these vehicles were quite a sight coming into the Canadian border towns of Windsor and Fort Erie, Ontario.

FARTHER AFIELD: INTO WEST GERMANY

Late in 1975, Oberkotter and vice chairman George Lamb acted on Casey's advice and formed a small executive group to look into expanding the ground service overseas into West Germany. A West German operation was not to be "international" in the sense of transporting packages between the United States and Germany, or between Germany and any of her European neighbors. Rather, this was to remain a domestic operation within Germany, UPS's first outside of North America.

There were four members of the group, each charged with evaluating a different aspect of launching UPS in West Germany. Among the team members were Joe Tranfo and Oz Nelson, who would become UPS's seventh chairman fifteen years later. Expanding service to West Germany was far from a done deal; if this group recommended against the idea it would likely be years before it resurfaced, particularly given the problems in Canada that had already cropped up.

Setting up headquarters in Düsseldorf in November 1975, the four were literally starting from scratch, without even any office supplies. They hired a clerk and found places to live. Two of them went to a stationery store and bought paper, pads, pens, and paper clips.

The group was aided by the German office of McKinsey & Company, the blue-chip consulting firm sometimes used by UPS in the United States to provide advice on specific initiatives. Not many people in West Germany had heard of UPS at the time, so the McKinsey connections in government and the private sector proved a convenient point of entrée to various decision makers. The four started traveling throughout the country, sometimes together but often apart, to visit various government officials and potential customers.

They met leaders of large and small businesses alike, and asked the questions they thought most important in deciding whether UPS should start a domestic West German operation: What are your weekly package delivery needs? What are the strengths and weaknesses of the Bundespost? Would you use this kind of service? How often? When the four would reconvene back in Düsseldorf from their visits, they kept reporting the same thing: the Bundespost, its would-be main competitor, didn't care much about service, paid little heed to the needs of its customers, and delivered packages on its terms, not its customers'. Its workers put in no overtime to deliver packages even one minute after quitting time, and there was nothing the customer could do about it.

For example, it often took weeks to receive a package around the holidays, and this parcel "service" included customers bringing packages or freight to the local train station and putting it on the train, with the recipient likewise having to go to a train station to claim the parcel. Fortunately for UPS, an opening in German law didn't automatically give the parcel monopoly to the Bundespost that the U.S. Postal Service enjoyed for first-class mail.

The Bundespost's vulnerability was just one of many factors that made West Germany attractive to UPS. Others included a relatively well-off population that was sending a huge volume of packages; an educated labor market; a developed zip code system; an excellent highway system that the UPS team was using to travel around the country; and a large and growing manufacturing base that UPS presciently foresaw could provide great customers for decades to come. Indeed, Germany is today the world's largest exporter, with $1 trillion in 2005 exports compared to $927.5 billion for the United States. Germany is UPS's biggest market outside of the United States.

The downside of expanding to West Germany in 1976? First, UPS knew that it was going to lose money in the short-term trying to build an operation in West Germany; it was just a question of how much. But when put into the context of the resources spent to fight the regulatory battles in the United States, the estimates of a few years of losses in the millions of dollars seemed eminently reasonable.

Second, there was also talk of organized resistance to UPS. According to Tranfo, UPS had been told by the McKinsey partners to expect some German pushback to letting a foreign-owned company set up operations and partner with some of the most recognizable German manufacturing names. Eventually, a consortium of seventeen small, local parcel delivery services banded together to organize protests against the foreign interloper.

But the people that mattered—German customers—clearly wanted an alternative to the Bundespost on one hand and mom-and-pop couriers on the other. No other American delivery company was yet on the scene. After about six months in Germany, the UPS working group gave its thumbs-up recommendation to the UPS board of directors in the spring of 1976. UPS would launch a domestic ground business in West Germany and there wasn't much time to get going. Packages were slated to start flowing in August.

GETTING STARTED

First things first. UPS needed vehicles to deliver packages; more precisely, it needed vehicle licenses. West Germany, at the time, issued trucking licenses using a similar model to one that New York City uses today to distribute taxi cab licenses. A certain number of licenses were allowed by policy, and once that limit was reached, more came "on the market" only when somebody else gave one up. A new company wanting to make a big splash could buy a batch of licenses—at an inflated rate no doubt—from companies that already owned them. The alternative was to start waiting the estimated thirty-year lead time for buying licenses. UPS decided to purchase as many licenses as it could.

The best way was to acquire a company that already had the licenses. A mom-and-pop freight forwarder called Stolze Brothers fit the bill. Stolze Brothers was based in a small town about twelve miles from Dortmund, the city where UPS planned on establishing its biggest operation. Though modest in scope, Stolze Brothers had plenty of both the red and blue trucking licenses that were issued at the time. The red licenses carried no restrictions on where a driver could go, while the blue licenses limited the truck to a certain radius of operation. The company also had several good trucking facilities that UPS could turn into hubs.

Blue and red were not the only colors that concerned UPS. There was also the "brown" question. While it hadn't occurred to UPS that its trademark color might be inappropriate for West Germany given the Brown Shirts of the Nazi regime, UPS heard from both potential customers and the McKinsey team that plain brown shirts on a driver might offend people. After some discussion, the company decided on dark tan shirts with light pinstripes. As it turned out, UPS might have spent less time considering shirt color and more on a crop of other cultural issues that undermined it those first few years.

UPS being UPS, the company started hiring people four months before the August day when packages would first be delivered, and by the time summer rolled around UPS Germany had more than 100 employees. Three future executives critical to the eventual success of UPS Germany were hired just a couple of months apart in 1976: Wolfgang Flick on July 19, Joerns Reineke on August 2, and Wolfgang Nast on August 30.

Flick, now the president of UPS Europe, hailed from the Giessen area, a main supply depot for the American military. His grandfather ran a one-man package delivery business in Giessen after World War II, using a single horse and wagon, which under the circumstances was probably more efficient than a car. According to Flick, there were very few working cars left in some parts of Germany at that point in time and very little fuel. Anyone in Giessen with a vehicle typically outfitted it with a wood-burning carburetor and a tiny chimney, the fumes from the burning wood powering the engine.

American soldiers stationed in Giessen would pass out candy

to Flick and his friends, and that simple act of kindness helped Flick think fondly of the United States in the years after, and the chance of joining an American company twenty-five years later was one he relished. "My early encounters with American soldiers kind of helped shape my view of the United States," Flick says.

Thirty years old in 1976, Flick saw a newspaper advertisement for a center manager at the new UPS center in Giessen. Not knowing exactly what kind of outfit UPS was, Flick showed up for his interview dressed in jeans and a T-shirt, while the UPS recruiters were all in suits. "I was certainly dressed wrong for the party," is how Flick puts it today.

In the United States in 1975, a young hotshot showing up for an interview to be a UPS manager in jeans and a T-shirt would have been—after being shown the door—a topic of "Can you believe that?" discussions for years. But given Flick's former apprenticeship and managerial experience at a wholesaling company in Giessen, together with UPS's desire to build the business quickly, he was hired right away.

Flick, still new to UPS, was puzzled that UPS drivers were so highly regarded in the United States. In West Germany, even among those who had gone through the German version of vocational training as opposed to university training, driving trucks was regarded as quite menial work, well below the status of someone with a formal apprenticeship under his belt like Flick himself, or craftsmen like carpenters, roof layers, or auto mechanics.

Still, after hearing so much about what a great company UPS was and getting firsthand seasoning in upstate New York, Flick anticipated preparing his own package center upon his return to Giessen. He was a little disappointed to find out that his place of business was set up in a former tavern littered with huge piles of bricks.

In August, however, right on schedule, package delivery operations in West Germany opened simultaneously in twelve cities across the western and northern parts of the country.

CULTURE CLASH

The company ran into immediate cultural problems with German drivers, not to mention the Italian and Turkish guest workers also included in the UPS driver workforce. Some were minor issues, such as a reluctance by Germans to be called by their first names and engage in other informalities. Others were more serious.

From the very start, relationships with employees were fraught with tension over the tremendous amount of work. Flick recalls telling drivers that they had, say, twenty-five stops that day, and that some drivers simply refused to work that much and walked out. Other drivers would go out on their routes and were never heard from again. "We hired a lot of people but we couldn't keep anyone on the payroll," Flick says.

It also didn't help that the employees were underpaid. Mindful of not losing too much money too soon, UPS in West Germany paid its drivers three or four marks less than drivers at other kinds of German companies, even though they had far more to do and logged many more driving miles. Due to the lack of customer density in those early days, drivers would have to sometimes drive hundreds of kilometers in the course of a day.

Reineke, as of late 2006 the district manager for Germany, remembers that one day at the outset of his delivery route, he quite by chance happened upon his father, who couldn't help but notice how few packages were in the vehicle. "Oh, is your work already done? Are you ready to come home?" he asked. Unfortunately, Reineke answered, he hadn't started yet. It wasn't the first time that Reineke's father, the mayor of the small town where they lived called Iserlohn, told him that UPS would never go anywhere.

Mike Eskew arrived late in 1976 to help design the West German transportation network, as the company obviously needed help creating better loads, combining driver deliveries, and devising more efficient ways to cover the areas they were serving. He had made his mark early on by doing just this kind of work first in Terre Haute, Indiana, and then at a new hub in Indianapolis. But all the reconfiguring of networks in the world couldn't change the fact that UPS had trouble hiring and keeping good employees. "Germany had minuscule unemployment, and generally if you didn't have a job, it was for a reason," Eskew says.

If getting drivers to work a full day was difficult enough, convincing them to put in overtime was nearly impossible. In those days in the nascent West German operation, drivers were expected to load their own packages in the morning, much like UPS businesses today in places like Poland and Turkey. There was no distinct "pre-load" staff. For the drivers, that meant getting to the package center quite early in the morning to load. Now the goal, of course, was that every package car be empty at the end of the day, which frequently meant staying until 7 P.M. or 7:30 P.M., which could make for some twelve-hour days.

Unbeknownst to UPS, it was uncommon in Germany to work overtime just to finish a job. Drivers continued to leave and take one of many other available jobs, with unemployment in West Germany at about four percent at the time.

All too ironically, then, the very same economic boom that made West Germany a good choice for UPS expansion had actually imperiled the entire operation. According to Flick, the company at one point in early 1977 ran an advertisement for drivers for six consecutive weeks in the classifieds of a local newspaper. It received not a single applicant. In fact, Eskew recalls that some drivers in West Germany would arrive at the package sorting center dressed in a suit and carrying a brief-case, then would dutifully change into their tan and pin-striped outfit once they arrived. "It obviously wasn't recognized as a professional job," he says.

For all its due diligence about the need for UPS-style customer service in West Germany, the four-person team hadn't anticipated issues associated with the demanding UPS culture, the West German bias against being a trucker, and the company's unwilling-ness to pay a premium for UPS-style employee devotion.

"It wasn't just differences in culture per se that were at work, but really how our kind of business was viewed, and that was as a bunch of truckers," Tranfo says. "And our working group didn't catch that while we were over there." After almost seventy years of UPS drivers being recognized as important members of American communities, objects of respect and affection, it came as a shock to UPS management back in Greenwich that the legendary driver culture could not be replicated in West Germany. And it wasn't just drivers who were leaving. In 1977 alone, Flick, transferred from Giessen to manage the bigger

Frankfurt operation, lost twelve full-time supervisors who didn't want to put up with the hours and low pay.

Despite the problems with employees and weak service in some areas, UPS had clearly hit upon a huge need in West Germany. For one thing, volume kept increasing. For another, in those instances when competent drivers actually completed their routes, customers loved the service, just like the executive working group predicted. That first holiday period in December 1976, for instance, Flick and/or one of his drivers would show up at a business with a package. Puzzled, the business owner or manager would frequently ask who, or what, UPS was and what manner of package it was delivering. According to Flick, it was only after the receipt was brought out that the customer would say something like that, "Oh, no wonder I didn't understand what you were bringing. I was expecting that to get here in about three weeks!"

After all, for customers, what was not to like? Here was a company that, from out of nowhere, arrived in West Germany and could blanket the northern half of the country with a one-day package delivery service. Already UPS was hearing from customers that planned to close warehouses and distribution centers because, if UPS could deliver their products in twenty-four or forty-eight hours to customers, what needed to be stored?

Wolfgang Nast, currently the UPS Europe Transportation manager, was another early employee, hired just a few weeks after packages started to be delivered. An acquaintance had told him about this "funny American company" that was challenging the Bundespost in delivering packages. Nast started on the 11 P.M. to 2 A.M. shift in UPS's biggest West German operation in Dortmund, unloading tractor-trailers, or "feeders" in UPS parlance.

Like Flick, Nast had come to the job with very few expectations of staying at UPS. When he first started unloading trailers, there were roughly 600 or 700 packages a night coming into the night sort, and the first few days he just wanted to do his job and leave. "You have to understand," Nast says, "before UPS came along in Germany, a truck driver was considered a low-class job. But you could immediately, or at least after a few weeks, see that UPS expected much more from all of us." Nast, like Flick, was amazed that this American company UPS had made an exact science of something the Bundespost did so poorly.

Well, not an exact science, as Nast himself proved. The package sorting center area was cramped, and Nast, who was a supervisor in the operation at that point, noticed that because packages came in and out of a single opening where the package cars pulled up and unloaded, the operation couldn't use a circular style conveyor system.

So, using a power saw one night, Nast sawed open a gaping hole in the wall and—voila—packages could be more easily routed into and out of the hub, the way a baggage conveyor works in an airport. "That was really our first important construction job in Germany," Nast says only half-jokingly. Eskew recalls that because of Nast's handiwork, "snow blew in one side of that building and out the other side," all winter. The engineering-oriented Nast and the engineer Eskew soon hit it off working nights together in Dortmund, discussing subjects dear to both, from zip codes of German cities to the best driving route from Dortmund to Hanover.

But years of growing pains still lay ahead.

There were other, early flaws in the West German operation

that, unlike the cultural issues, would have been very easy to fix if only the company had had its eyes wide open. Among them: UPS decided to give drivers U.S.-style benefits, with the right to earn fifteen or sometimes twenty days of vacation, while a typical German vacation was twenty-eight or thirty days from the day that a worker starts. Also, the UPS ownership concept came under fire, because certain kinds of stock ownership played havoc with a West German worker's pension. "You saw a lot of 'we are UPS, we know what's best for you,' even though the point they were making did not really apply to Germany," Flick says. "Had I not been to the United States and seen how a UPS operation could work when it was running at top-speed, I think I would have really lost faith."

Even UPS's vaunted, tried-and-true promotion from within philosophy backfired in West Germany. When UPS started in West Germany, new employees were told that one of the great, decidedly American aspects about the company was the upward mobility. UPS, of course, was run—and still is run—on the premise that hard-working, resourceful drivers and package loaders and dock workers can become supervisors, and that the best supervisors can become managers. But much more so than in the United States, many Europeans at that time, and West Germans in particular, were suspicious of easy professional mobility. Most line workers, drivers, or other blue-collar workers would never expect to be promoted into a company's management.

The result was that some employees with potential at UPS in West Germany refused promotions because they didn't feel comfortable with managing their friends or taking on more responsibility. On the other hand, some employees were so amazed at the possibility of promotion that they wanted one right away. In

1977 in Frankfurt, where he took on a manager role less than one year after the company started in West Germany, Flick had employees coming up to him unsolicited, insisting on being made a supervisor. "I said, 'Sorry, we can't have just bosses,'" Flick says. Because the promotion-from-within philosophy wasn't working, UPS had to bring in more American managers than it wanted to, which just started the whole cycle of unrealistic expectations and cultural misunderstanding all over again. In the long run, however, the policy did take hold.

The amount of opportunity and trust given to those who did succeed caused early German employees like Reineke, Nast, and Flick to fully embrace the company. Flick even told his wife that he had found the company where he would spend the rest of his working life. She asked how he could possibly know that, given the problems he was having managing the workload and his employees. "I told her that I just knew running something like this, trying to make it work, impressing customers with good service, was perfect for me," Flick says.

Before long, the embattled UPS employees who stuck around developed a sort of defiant us-against-them team spirit. The Bundespost was delivering scores as many packages as UPS was, and certainly wasn't going to sit by as the newcomer poached its customers. It decided to use its natural advantages, beating UPS's rates and touting its own comprehensive national coverage.

The assertion that the Bundespost exploited its official capacity as steward of Germany's telephone service was just the beginning of a thirty-year debate between UPS and the German and EU authorities concerning exactly what constituted fair competition. UPS expanding into Europe moved the issue of just how aggressively a national government should compete with the private sector from the United States to Europe.

AN AVALANCHE OF PACKAGES

UPS's strategy to expand has served it well for a century. One could quibble with the timing of entering a state here or a city there, but for the most part UPS grew chiefly through successful—although certainly arduous—geographic expansion. It seemed only natural in 1978, then, after having conquered all of America and aggressively pursuing expansion into more provinces in Canada, that UPS in West Germany should branch out and serve customers in the southern half of the country.

While the West German business was struggling when it was decided to expand to the whole of the country, competitive realities didn't leave UPS a lot of choice. For example, one of its big service problems was that customers ready to embrace UPS balked when they found out that UPS only served certain portions of the country. According to Eskew, when trying to win a client over, UPS salespeople would have to say, "Yes, we can take those packages; no, we can't take those; we don't serve that town either, sorry."

The difference between U.S. expansion and West Germany expansion, though, was that the U.S. network was typically primed and ready for more packages to be fed into the system. The only tough part about managing U.S. expansion was having enough trained managers to go in and run new districts, new package sorting centers, and new hubs.

In West Germany, by contrast, the UPS network wasn't ready for a heavy influx of new packages throughout the country, and once it started accepting them it couldn't exactly stop. As former international chief Don Layden puts it: "You can't just say to customers, 'On second thought, we are not delivering packages today.'" In order for the West German business to try to prepare for this avalanche of packages, Ed Bolton, the American who was leading UPS in West Germany, and Eskew decided that they had to break down every driver route and explain to the driver how to serve it. The main goal, according to Eskew, was to avoid drivers crisscrossing a city to deliver packages. Within one area of a city they could deliver in pretty much any order they wanted. But UPS didn't want them wasting time going back and forth between areas.

On one of his subsequent driver rides to test quality levels, Eskew was with a driver who spoke no English, and Eskew's new German was shaky. The driver proceeded to deliver a package and return to a specific hotel after every delivery, then deliver the next package. This went on a few times. "Why do we keep returning to this hotel?" Eskew finally asked in German. The driver replied: "I was a cab driver and I can get anywhere in the city from this hotel."

By the time Eskew returned to the United States at the end of 1978, UPS provided service to cities all over West Germany. In the two years following the expansion, UPS's West German volume numbers grew rapidly, and by the time 1980 rolled around the company had experienced 500 percent growth in revenues over the first four years, averaging about 75,000 parcels a day, compared with the Bundespost's 900,000. However, UPS was losing money, and lots of it, as the investment to build the national network wasn't recouped by the new volume.

TURNAROUND

In the late 1970s, UPS quantified its German and Canadian operational losses in cents per share, the thinking being, as Layden says, "If you say we lost one million dollars this quarter it sounds like a lot of money, but one cent a share doesn't sound as important."

But accounting niceties couldn't obscure the obvious. A chorus of UPS managers from all over the country chimed in, asking why UPS was in Europe in the first place if it couldn't make any money there. "Questions arose in many people's minds, including amongst the board and the outside directors," Layden says. "The perception of the typical UPS manager in the United States was that we had to do something to stop the losses, and if we couldn't stop the losses, we should get out of there."

Layden met George Lamb on a Saturday morning at the UPS office in Greenwich, Connecticut. Lamb asked him to go to Germany to do a study on how to salvage the Germany operations, if they could be salvaged.

What followed turned out to be a case study in turning around an underperforming outpost. Layden and his team talked to a rival shipper and department store clients. They rode with drivers and shadowed managers. They met with government officials. "You could see that a lot of the local German nationals were more than willing," Layden says. "And they just hadn't been trained correctly."

The team evaluated everything from the drivers' uniforms to delivery rates to salaries. After two different trips to West Germany, the team came up with five key recommendations:

- Salaries had to be increased across the board, and in some cases nearly doubled (this was the hardest recommendation for the UPS board to accept, although Lamb bought into it immediately)

- A large team of American managers, drivers, and trainers needed to come to West Germany and re-train their West German counterparts

- West Germans needed to be trained to take charge of the operation as quickly as possible, and then be held accountable for the operation's performance

- An American regional manager must live in West Germany

- The American regional manager should report directly to the chief operating officer (Jack Rogers), as the company's other regional managers did, rather than to a separate international UPS president

The board accepted the findings unanimously. Salaries were doubled in short order. One of the immediate results of the compensation was a major upgrade in the driver job candidates. Assigning American managers and drivers to train their counterparts was also a masterstroke. Drivers trained drivers, managers trained managers. "The drivers were really trained in the right methods, but not *just* methods," Flick says. "They drilled into us why service was so important, that it could be a competitive advantage."

The cultural chasm was also bridged. For example, future UPS International president Ron Wallace introduced American tackle football to his German co-workers, organizing a league and playing wide receiver for the UPS team.

In another move, the company assigned a forty-year veteran from the United States to shadow Joerns Reineke for six months, as Reineke had been promoted to center manager. One day in deep winter, the treacherous black ice on the roads made the going slow and difficult. But there were no UPS accidents and no package returns. The old-timer told Reineke to go out and buy a grill and some hot dogs, hamburgers, and pieces of chicken for a mid-winter barbecue. Reineke had been introduced to the management idea that off-beat rewards can make hard work seem more enjoyable.

Another unusual aspect of UPS management that the American managers spent time on, according to Nast, was employee empathy. The UPS management culture of nurturing an individual's career and viewing the worker as an individual with his or her own strengths and weaknesses was not a widely shared management philosophy at the time in West Germany, where blue-collar workers, especially, were expected to just put their time in.

It wasn't just the Americans who traveled across the ocean; West Germans came over to the United States as well. Nast, for example, went to Philadelphia in 1982 to work in that district, and Wolfgang Flick would become head of the UPS Utah district.

All of these efforts helped UPS Germany stop hemorrhaging

money, although it would be many more years before it entered the black. After more than thirty years, it's one of UPS's strongest areas of the world and a healthy contributor to global profitability. Turning around West Germany was also important psychologically for UPS, because it needed the institutional confidence to take future risks.

More practically, it kept UPS on pace to build a European network that would eventually prove to be ahead of its time in many ways. During the next two decades borders in Europe would be effectively erased, the Berlin Wall would fall, the Internet would emerge, and further globalization would occur, all of which meant that the network that was being built during the 1970s and 1980s in Germany would eventually be utilized far beyond anyone's imagination. And just like UPS's network in the United States, the German roots that UPS put down would prove difficult for any other company to replicate.

UPS RULES FOR THE ROAD

Beyond the Golden Link:
Going International

- **Leave no stone unturned.** When UPS faced chronic underperformance in its foray into Germany in the late 1970s, it created a task force that reached out to rival shippers, department store clients, and other customers. Members of the team rode with drivers and shadowed managers. Everything from driver uniforms to delivery rate to salaries was evaluated, and the team issued key recommendations that helped jumpstart UPS performance in Germany.

- **Think global, act local.** When UPS started to build its global network, it brought district managers working abroad together to discover the best carriers, locate strategic partners, and scout out local attorneys who could structure deals. The knowledge these allies provided about the local markets helped develop UPS's operations in those difficult early days.

6

Creating a Truly Global Business

"When we decided to expand globally, we had two choices. We could go very slowly . . . or we could kick the doors down."

—OZ NELSON,
UPS CEO, 1990–1996

David Abney, UPS COO, keeps on a wall in his office a large, colorful map of the world. The eyes of an American visitor instinctively dart to the central spot that the United States typically occupies on a map but, oddly, the most dominant economic and military power in world history is nowhere to be found.

Abney clearly relishes the U.S.–centric confusion as the visitor slowly realizes that this particular map—marketed as the "What's Up? South!" map by its manufacturer—stands the world, as it were, on its head. Instead of the traditional north to south orientation featured on classroom maps from Seattle to Sarasota, this one presents the southern hemisphere as the top half of the map. After all, who ever said north was up, anyway? The uncomfortably inverted United States and China, robbed of their mystique, appear as just mere land masses, initially as unrecognizable as the scores of other countries that Americans can't find on a map.

"The United States doesn't look so important viewed from what we think of as an upside-down perspective, and out of the central part of the map," Abney says. This is just one technique that Abney uses to remind his UPS management committee colleagues that it's a big world out there, and that assumptions of what lies down the road are only that: guesses.

Indeed, looking at the way a simple map can jar firmly held worldviews leaves one with the impression that maybe one of the great debates in the business world today—which country will become the next great economic superpower—is perhaps also a matter of perspective.

Much of the current focus centers on the might of China and the potential of India, for example, but why not focus on India's potential first and China's manufacturing heft second? After all, it really just depends on how far into the future the prognosticators want to look, and from what angle. Maybe a country such as Brazil, with its incredible stock of natural resources and young, highly educated workforce of 150 million, is really the place to watch over the next fifty years. And for that matter what about Europe, which has about one-half the population of China but far more members of an educated middle class?

Then there is Russia, which seemingly had so much potential after the breakup of the Soviet Union, but which has failed to build a transparent, workable marketplace that international investors can trust. UPS has targeted Russia for fourteen years, and as Abney says, "We have been waiting fourteen years for something to happen infrastructure-wise." But what if UPS had 140 years to wait?

And what about the idea of the United States not just being relegated to the fringes in Abney's map, but displaced from its perch at the nexus of global economic activity as well? A world without the United States in the starring economic role can be troubling even to those missionaries of the global order, a new world in which the United States leads only in the category of accrued debt. Even at the UPS-sponsored biannual economic and trade conference called Longitudes, where urbane awareness of the coming new global power rankings rules the day, conference attendees worry about what the United States can do to stay in front.

While the United States itself faces tough economic competition over the next few decades, UPS likely will be well-positioned no matter what happens, due to forward-thinkers like Abney. As of late 2006, UPS concentrates on twenty-three countries, according to Abney (focus intently on any more than that, the thinking goes, and one could be pouring resources into a black hole). No matter which of those twenty-three countries becomes the new hot spot, it doesn't matter so much to UPS management. "What is obvious to us at UPS," says Frank Sportolari, UPS vice president of European Strategy as of late 2006, "is that global trade is increasing everywhere. Whether it's India, Brazil, or China, we are going to facilitate global commerce."

BEYOND INTERNATIONAL SERVICE

In 1985, UPS was anything but a global company. The full extent of its international operations ten years after obtaining full interstate rights in the U.S. was a domestic ground operation in Canada and a domestic ground operation in West Germany. A package could not be sent from New York to London via UPS. Paris to Frankfurt? Forget it. UPS was still three years from starting operations in Turkey. UPS had no flights into and no service to China, which was just re-emerging as a player in the global economy.

The company's scars from the first few years in West Germany, in particular, were still healing. "In a strange way, our West Germany experience was valuable because it showed us what *not* to do," Tranfo says. "Most operations after that resulted from an acquisition, a joint venture, or an agent relationship."

Indeed, the problems launching the domestic operation in West Germany would inform how UPS would operate on a global stage for the next three decades. There was to be a critical difference, however, in how UPS would go about applying the hard-won lessons from West Germany to its operations in Europe and Asia.

After a series of initial agent relationships, Europe would essentially grow by acquisition. The UPS presence in Asia, though, would largely be developed through a series of joint ventures and long-term agent relationships. Joint ventures, while necessary in markets such as China that mandated them, turned out to be the method with the most complications, as UPS eventually spent years and many millions of dollars extricating itself from joint ventures that had ceased to serve any useful purpose.

The difference between an agency relationship, such as the one with Unsped in Turkey, and a joint venture is that in a joint venture both investment and profit are shared, perhaps not fifty-fifty, but shared nonetheless. In an agent scenario the host company makes as much money as it can for itself while also sponsoring and managing a UPS operation. In Turkey, for example, UPS doesn't get a dime of Unsped's profits made outside of the UPS Turkey operation.

It's not surprising, given the structural differences in how UPS Europe and UPS Asia developed, that UPS operates in two distinctly different ways in Germany and China, its two biggest offshore markets. UPS Germany boasts an extensive domestic ground network, while in China all domestic service is still express and delivered mostly through the air.

ANOTHER ADAPTATION FOR UPS

Back in 1985, though, the only certainty was that UPS had to adapt again, as it had so many times in the past. It was facing challenges in its core U.S. domestic business from Roadway Package System, its U.S. Next Day Air product volume still lagged far behind FedEx's, and UPS domestic clients expanding overseas had no choice but to use FedEx, DHL, or another service.

Yet, despite its woeful beginnings in West Germany, that business was finally beginning to show promise. Further international expansion was clearly the solution for growing the business, a conclusion that FedEx and DHL had already come to for their own companies. UPS was faced with two choices when it wanted to expand beyond West Germany and Canada. "We could go very slowly, and we might be looking at twenty-five years or so," says former CEO Oz Nelson. "Or we could kick the doors down."

Kicking the doors down would mean losing money in the

short-term as the company set up offices, brought over managers and their families, built infrastructure, and marketed its services to clients who might never have heard of UPS.

The advantage that UPS had over FedEx was that as a privately held company, its owners were the employees and retirees. While these stakeholders might not always be 100 percent happy with the course UPS management charted, they knew better than to expect results in two or three quarters and were used to taking a longer-term view.

When UPS decided to expand beyond West Germany in Europe in 1985, the first step was to choose where to expand to. The management committee decided on the U.K., which had been the runner-up after West Germany back in 1976, as well as France, the Netherlands, Belgium, and Luxembourg, four countries whose proximity to West Germany would allow them to quickly get packages to a yet-to-be-determined West German hub.

And if UPS was not going to start service from scratch akin to West Germany, it also had to decide just how it would build a presence in these countries. According to Nelson, vice chairman at the time, the company brought its district managers together and announced that the time was right to go beyond West Germany and Canada. UPS assigned several of these managers, some of whom had never before ventured outside of the United States, to go visit the biggest package shippers in France, Belgium, the Netherlands, Luxembourg, and the U.K., and determine how much they were paying for what kinds of services. Who were they using? Why? How much were they shipping? They were also told to find out who the best carriers were, to locate robust partners who knew the local market and were interested in being part of something big.

Nelson also encouraged the managers to scout out local attorneys who could help structure the deals, whether they ended up being agency agreements or some other type of partnership. "We told them to find someone to buy, someone to partner with, whatever it took," Nelson says. As Sportolari says, "Those local companies had far more knowledge about the local markets than we could have had."

LAUNCHING INTERNATIONAL SERVICE

Charlie Adams, who led UPS's Asia Pacific region from 1994-2003, was a TWA executive in 1985. He remembers UPS representatives calling and telling him that they were thinking of starting four international intra-Europe lanes connecting Luxembourg, Paris, London, and Brussels with a potential air hub in Frankfurt, and would TWA be interested in becoming UPS's first international air express carrier? "My logic at TWA was actually that UPS was so disciplined that our operations would be forced to get better, and if we got better we could charge our customers more," Adams said. "So I was all for it." But Adams, and UPS, both proved overconfident.

For starters, there were problems maintaining enough package volume in all three main routes: from Europe to the United States; from the United States to Europe; and between the five European countries. When it kicked off the international air service among the United States and Europe, UPS failed to align its service offerings with potential customers. It was, ironically, the exact opposite set of problems from those the company faced with its domestic ground service in West Germany ten years earlier, when UPS had the right product but no efficient way of providing it. Now it had a trusted agent in five European countries and its own strong base in another, but also a set of expensive, premium services that customers were not responding to because their value had not been made explicit.

Not only did European businesses exhibit little demand for all the different service options that UPS presented, but they showed even less stomach for the prices. UPS failed to make the case as to why European customers had to get their products from Paris to London overnight, or from Brussels to New York in two days when the Belgium Post did it in four days for far less money. FedEx famously convinced the American business community that it needed overnight package delivery service, but business conditions in the United States were primed for that service. Not so in Europe.

Customers also received conflicting answers about UPS's services and prices. "It wasn't a very efficient system," Nelson says. "A lot of the packages we sent from Europe to the United States, and within Europe, were misclassified at first." In addition, because of European taxes, customs duties, and other added charges that UPS didn't plan for when shipping between countries, the company often badly underpriced deliveries. "We really had no idea what the market was," says Nast, a hub manager in West Germany at the time. "We started marketing international delivery to customers who did some business in the United States, but it was very unscientific."

In response, CEO Rogers and Nelson encouraged UPS managers to work with customers to glean firsthand knowledge and understanding of customer needs. "It took some time for us to actually listen to the marketplace," Nelson says.

While the product rollout was mishandled, other issues cropped up that would have been more difficult to anticipate. Due to the large American armed forces contingent in West Germany, for example, the Deutsche Post co-opted airlines around the holidays to carry mail. So UPS had a very hard time getting planes to fly packages to America during the holidays.

There were also cultural challenges with employees. British and French employees were used to drinking alcohol at lunch, and it was impossible to make employees of a UPS agent toe the UPS line. Clearing customs was another major problem. In 1986, any package crossing a European border had to be brokered, and UPS and other couriers had to pay a Value Added Tax (VAT).

The local agents proved invaluable. They taught UPS how to work with customs, smoothed over problems with employees, and even made recommendations about how to better structure UPS's European hub-and-spoke model. Says Wolfgang Flick, who took charge of the Cologne air hub in 1986, "It turned out that the agents were very often right about local issues. It was really the first time I learned to rely on people who were not my own handpicked managers."

PINPOINTING A EUROPEAN HUB

During one meeting about customs issues, Flick, then an IE manager on the Cologne expansion team, drafted a flow chart that discussed how to more efficiently get express air packages through customs. At the end of the meeting the ranking UPSer in the meeting announced, "Okay, it looks like Wolfgang is the one to run this."

He embraced the challenge. One thing that had become clear to Flick in the first year of international air express was that using Frankfurt as a hub was a mistake. Frankfurt had a night curfew on flights, something a city like Cologne, for example, didn't have. The Cologne airport was tiny, really more an airstrip than an airport, though it included a few storage sheds and even a nine-hole golf course.

But part of the beauty of Cologne was its utter lack of infrastructure, because UPS could build its European air hub any way it saw fit. Flick understood that what UPS needed given the scope of its ambitions was an air network that not only brought all European packages going to the United States into one convenient location, but that could also serve as a base for future growth. Already, in addition to the international delivery service, UPS had launched in West Germany domestic air service, as well. For those particular flights the company often used Cessna 404s, taking out the seats for package space and even stuffing deliveries into the nose compartments and tiny little wing compartments, where an extra package or two could fit.

During the 1986 holiday season, Lufthansa, which had replaced TWA as UPS's main common carrier for international deliveries, threw UPS a wicked curve ball. It couldn't provide a plane because it needed it for its own cargo.

UPS immediately dispatched a DC-8 from its U.S. domestic network and flew it from the U.S. to Cologne on December 23, 1986, in time to deliver for Christmas. Even though the plane was barely half full, UPS felt it was important to show that its customer service was, as UPS promised, better than that of Deutsche Post. "We did whatever it took to show our European customers that we take our commitments seriously," Flick said about the episode.

A CHANGING STRATEGY TO TAKE ON THE WORLD

Just as UPS felt it was its "manifest destiny," so to speak, to expand throughout the United States, Canada, and West Germany, management decided in 1988 that it couldn't halt its international expansion with Western Europe. "I think at the very top there was an understanding that we had to be a global company," says Layden, who led UPS International from 1988 through 1994. "We were clearly behind DHL and progressively behind FedEx."

Layden believed a shift in strategy was also needed. UPS had tried starting from scratch in West Germany. It had tried setting up agent relationships in five other Western European countries. Both had proven painful. Now Layden wanted to try another approach to "kicking the door down." Why not acquire companies that had already taken off the door hinges and supplied the ramming rod that could knock the door down? As Layden says, "The other methods were proving to take too long to get profitable, so the thought was to buy companies outright." UPS had actually tried to take the acquisition route in a big way a couple of years earlier. In 1986, it conducted serious discussions with DHL about acquiring that company to give UPS a global presence in one fell swoop. Under that scenario, Layden would become the head of operations for the operation after it was integrated into UPS.

Layden, for his part, couldn't wait. At age fifty-four, he probably could have called it a career. But he had served as corporate director of human resources for eight years and was itching to return to operations, and there was no operational challenge bigger than building UPS's global package delivery network. After the DHL talks broke down over a number of sticking points, UPS business development manager John Alden put together a team to look into how to further expand globally. Alden's group subsequently joined Layden's group that had been slated to run the acquired DHL operation. Just like that, Layden had his operational mandate, which was to build an international UPS network that could serve customers on a global scale.

FROM THREE TO 180 COUNTRIES SERVED

Instead of agency agreements, Layden was determined to acquire successful local couriers. While the agency agreements had taken UPS to a certain level, he and Rogers felt that to really build a common product portfolio and provide the same level of service everywhere, UPS had to own the companies. In the years hence, incidentally, UPS has shown that it can work in many different ways around the globe, and that execution—not necessarily structure—is the most important variable to get right.

Layden's first goal was to acquire companies in Western Europe where UPS currently maintained an agent relationship, and then move on to the rest of Europe, Asia, and then the less strategic (for UPS) parts of the world. Over the next four years, UPS made sixteen major European acquisitions, as well as two major acquisitions that brought service to many parts of Asia, the Middle East, and Africa. Important joint venture relationships were forged in China, Japan, and Korea, and agent relationships were set up with Unsped in Turkey and several other countries.

In Europe, the newly acquired companies often dwarfed the size of the agent that UPS had been doing business with. In France, for example, UPS had 400 people under its banner when it acquired a company with 2,500 employees. Some key acquisitions, such as CarryFast in Britain, quickly became headaches for UPS because, moneymakers before being acquired, they lost money as UPS tried to overlay UPS infrastructure and policies.

In addition, many of these acquired companies had vastly different IT systems that couldn't "talk" to one another, so UPS had trouble tracking packages from one European country to another. Customs would often hold packages for days and neither the sender nor the consignee would know where the delivery was—and sometimes UPS wouldn't either.

Throughout this period, UPS tried to shore up its European operations by acquiring companies with the capabilities to solve some of the problems it was having. For example, in July 1990 UPS announced the acquisition of the $26 million Seabourne European Express Parcels, a British express company with hubs in England, France, Spain, Sweden, and the Netherlands. Seabourne had a reputation as a company especially adept at handling cross-border trucking transactions and moving packages through customs very quickly. The result of these strong ground acquisitions in Europe was a clear competitive advantage for UPS; for while its competitors focused almost exclusively on air express from major European cities, UPS was building the first-ever integrated air and ground European network.

The landmark acquisition in Asia, in 1988, was Asian Courier

Systems (ACS), a company of about 200 people based in Hong Kong with coverage in Malaysia, Hong Kong, Singapore, Taiwan, and Thailand. In Singapore, ACS had 600 square feet in space rented out in a factory building. But it did have many good customers that it served on its distinctive Toyota brown scooters, thanks to Singapore's strong manufacturing bent then particularly in electronic semiconductors.

The acquisition that expanded UPS's service the most, by sheer number of countries, was a British-based global delivery company called IML in 1988. IML was attractive because it had very experienced managers who knew how to get packages into very hard-to-get-to places all over Africa and the Middle East through its own agents in those regions. "In terms of the scope and scale of our global expansion, IML got us from about forty-five countries to almost two hundred," says retired UPS COO John Beystehner.

By the end of 1989, UPS served more than 175 countries and territories. While expanding into Western Europe had required separate acquisitions, UPS had acquired huge chunks of territory around the world through ACS and IML. By the time Jack Rogers retired and Nelson took the CEO helm in 1990, the plan to expand around the world had been largely completed, but it was tenuous coverage at best, and outside of the United States, a nonprofitable one. Rogers and vice chairman Nelson had said they were ready to lose more than $1 billion launching the international business, and clearly they were well on their way.

At one point in the early 1990s, the company was losing money so fast that there was talk of abandoning the European expansion altogether, just as there had been talk a decade earlier about scuttling the domestic West German business.

David Abney remembers the doubts about the young international business, saying that the premium, express volume that UPS had anticipated didn't materialize. "In the late 1980s there was a real question as to whether UPS should pull the plug on the effort to go global," Abney says. "The issue was what kind of volume we were getting and how much it was costing to move that volume."

BABY STEPS IN ASIA

Yet, UPS plowed ahead. While the company was establishing a strong presence in Europe, it was falling behind the competition just about everywhere else. Despite the impressive number of countries served, the fact remained that in many of the most important markets, UPS had made the fewest inroads.

China, in particular, was starting to stir. Despite Richard Nixon's much-vaunted overture to China in 1972, the country essentially remained closed until 1978. It wasn't until the mid-1980s that a tremendous flow of foreign investment spurred the manufacturing capacity that China is known for today.

FedEx started working with agents in China in 1984, and in 1989 acquired Flying Tigers, an international air cargo carrier, giving it routes all over Asia and further inroads into China. In 1987, FedEx also got the jump on UPS in Japan when it was approved by the U.S. Department of Transportation to launch a U.S.-to-Japan express delivery service.

DHL, of course, had been doing business in Asia since 1972. In 1969, three Americans started DHL in California, with an eye toward Asia. First they flew documents from California to

Hawaii, then moved westward across Asia. The Australian company TNT Express arrived in Asia shortly after that and eventually built a healthy 20 percent market share.

In 1987, UPS acted and formed an agency agreement with Sinotrans, the default government-owned company that partnered with all the major Western couriers to some degree. DHL and TNT both had agreements with Sinotrans, while FedEx had abandoned its arrangement with Sinotrans and was in the midst of a series of relationships with different government-owned delivery companies.

Down in Hong Kong and Singapore, the ACS acquisition was finalized in July 1988. Even before any expatriate Americans arrived in Hong Kong or Singapore, ACS employees started getting suspicious that individual Americans might not know that much about Singapore. Mary Yeo, who would rise to be the country manager in UPS Singapore, was a sales executive for ACS in Singapore then. She recalls opening up a huge UPS shipment from the United States and finding boxloads of toilet paper, and wondering what other misconceptions UPS managers held about Southeast Asia.

American expatriates arrived for several weeks in October 1988 to train the ACS staff in UPS methods and practices. Since its colonial connection to the U.K., Singapore has always been a haven of sorts for the Western traveler, as witnessed by its famous old hotels, such as Raffles. In 1988, though, Singapore, just a causeway away from Malaysia and a ferry ride to Indonesia, was not yet the renowned center of finance that it is today. To the newly arrived American UPS employees, it was undoubtedly a strange place with an opaque culture.

"To put it mildly, there was some culture shock on both sides," Yeo says. Most of the American contingent had never been outside of the United States before, according to Yeo, much less witnessed Muslim employees wearing headdresses and veils. One UPS manager insisted on grasping the hand of a woman employee who was visibly uncomfortable shaking hands with a man. Each day the local staff would run out to try to find salads for the Americans who wouldn't touch any of the curries or other Singaporean specialties.

The UPS way of working was as stifling to the local staff as the Singapore heat was for the visitors. It took local employees hours to get their expense reports done correctly under the rigorous UPS procedures. "I used a lot of white-out in those days," Yeo says. "You couldn't make an error or all the paperwork would come back to you." The Americans showed up for work every day sweltering in their dark suits, insisting that the local staff do the same in a country eighty miles from the equator. One Saturday working at the hub, Yeo showed up in jeans and a T-shirt and was sent home to change into business attire.

Even though the ACS acquisition was UPS's passport to parts of Southeast Asia, that entrée did not necessarily guarantee tight, profitable operations. Adams recalls that the ACS Bangkok offices operated out of a house into the early 1990s. In Malaysia, ACS had a very impressive domestic operation, moving 50,000–60,000 pieces per month, and the country manager there wanted to build a bigger building. The only problem was that the operation was losing money on each piece it handled. In other words, the more volume it did, the more money the company lost.

UPS operations in Japan were also sputtering. In 1992, Adams, who left TWA to go to work for UPS in London, was sent to Tokyo to try to jumpstart the struggling joint venture between UPS and Yamato, the premier Japanese parcel delivery company. The joint venture, called Unistar, began operating in November 1990, just a couple of years after UPS entered the Asian market through its acquisition of ACS. Unistar was owned 50 percent by UPS and 50 percent by Yamato, and had yet to turn a profit.

In fact, the Unistar joint venture embodied the range of issues UPS was having throughout its international business: cultural issues, brand issues, volume issues. The previous year, UPS international operations had lost $213 million, according to a filing with the SEC. The only profitable operation was its domestic German business. A number of people, according to Layden, questioned whether UPS's international operations would ever be profitable. According to Layden: "I got flak from just about everywhere except the CEO suite."

Such heavy losses in many organizations would not have been tolerated, but UPS's ownership by employees carried the day, as managers knew they were in it for the long term. There were no Wall Street expectations to meet, no skeptical or angry outside investors to placate. "A lot of people at UPS in the 1980s knew that we had to turn into a global organization," Adams says. "But when it got into 1992, 1993, 1994, 1995, and still losing money, I think a lot of people were wondering what we had gotten ourselves into."

FedEx was not immune to the market forces affecting UPS. The need to placate Wall Street led it to announce in March 1992 a massive pullback in Europe, halting deliveries between European countries and laying off more than 6,000 workers. FedEx has never fully recovered in Europe.

THE MAKINGS OF A TURNAROUND

Despite the fact that UPS was still not making money on its international service, Nelson and Layden did see some positive signs for future growth. Early on in Europe and Asia, UPS relied on its United States recipe for success, which was to have significant fixed costs and then push as much volume as possible through the system. But slowly UPS started to slim down its operation and push some of its excess, unprofitable volume out of the system, finding a better mix of express and cargo freight.

In 1995 and 1996, in fact, UPS had negative volume growth in its Asia Pacific region, something that didn't look good in press releases but that was necessary. Tom Murphy, head of UPS air operations in Asia as of late 2006 and a protégé of Adams at TWA and then UPS, had been selling airfreight space on Browntails for some time, going for the Holy Grail of a 100 percent load rate. In the late 1980s and early 1990s, UPS was flying with a thirty percent or forty percent express load, with the rest being filled with freight. But as time went on and UPS built the express service, according to Murphy, premium-priced express packages were gradually replacing the freight. "You know, running airplanes takes a lot of money," Murphy says. "So the more you can fill planes with your premium products, the better you are going to do."

THE BORDERS FALL IN EUROPE

In 1989, Annette Storr was a college student in Berlin. Today a member of UPS Europe's public affairs office, Storr recalls peering through a crack in the Berlin Wall that she was hammering at with thousands of others on that historic November day in 1989. An East German guard stood looking straight-faced until he finally broke down and relaxed as Storr and her friends climbed over the Wall into no-man's-land and talked to him for a few minutes.

In the same way that German reunification eventually created new problems for the country after the initial euphoria, so too did a newly powerful Deutsche Post continue to cause problems for UPS in the early 1990s. UPS repeatedly claimed that the German government-owned postal service used its monopoly on regular mail to subsidize a series of high-tech hubs that were used to sort packages, and that it never could have made that kind of investment without being subsidized by its government monopoly. In 1994, the EU ruled in UPS's favor in one suit, agreeing that the Deutsche Post used its monopoly on first-class mail to illegally subsidize competition against private carriers.

In Germany, it wasn't only the Berlin Wall that was destined to fall. UPS, as well as Deutsche Post and FedEx for that matter, received some good news in 1996 when the EU passed legislation that effectively removed borders between EU members, meaning that UPS trucks, package cars, and vans could move from country to country without having to clear packages through customs. For UPS, this meant that its hard-won pan-European ground network, developed while its competitors emphasized air express, could operate far more efficiently. More good news followed with a watershed moment for UPS in Germany when it introduced its automated ground hub in Frankfurt in 1997. It used cutting-edge, European-designed package sorting technology that would be employed in Worldport several years later.

All of these factors in Asia and Europe coalesced. With increasing express volume, fewer costs clearing customs, and more efficient package sorting systems, UPS's international business was finally profitable in 1998, making operating profits of $56 million.

The globalization embodied in the opening of European borders was followed by an even larger-scale removal of barriers: the explosion of online retail. In 1999 express air profits, fueled by Internet orders, continued to drive profits for UPS International. By 2000, the Internet and globalization sparked a huge increase in premium packages within Europe. The volume was growing at twenty percent each year, and the big strategic accounts were growing especially fast. According to Paul White, UPS Europe's vice president of marketing at the time, the revenues really exploded when the most lucrative UPS customers—those small-to-medium five-package-per-day customers that get only small discounts—started to order via the Internet as well.

Perhaps not coincidentally, the UPS driver ethos so well known in the United States started to penetrate Europe as UPS became more and more successful there. For example, in 1986, when Frank Sportolari told colleagues at a former employer that he was leaving to take a job at UPS as an IT specialist, they were disappointed for him. "That's too bad," one of his colleagues replied. "Weren't they hiring drivers?"

THE OPPORTUNITY OF A LIFETIME: UPS IN CHINA

The improvement in Europe in the mid-1990s was mirrored by success in Asia as well. By 1994, the air express market in

Asia was growing at upward of 20 percent each year, and by 1996 the Asia Pacific region was in the black. Except for the Asia financial crisis in 1998, profits have progressed every year since.

In November 2000, UPS hopes in China were greatly improved when the U.S. Department of Transportation selected UPS as the fourth U.S. carrier with rights into China, joining FedEx, Northwest Airlines, and United Airlines. But it still needed a new air hub to take advantage of this new status. In 2001, UPS chose a relative dark horse in the competition, Clark Air Force base in the Philippines, due to the Philippines' "open-skies" policy and the strategic location of Clark.

The geographical center of Asia is not China, Singapore, or Japan, but the Philippines. Most Asian countries are within a two- or three-hour flight of the Philippines, four at the most. While FedEx's Asian air hub is also in the Philippines, at Subic Bay, that location's short airstrip makes for a tough landing in bad weather. Clark, on the other hand, is positioned in a valley, protected from the Philippines' stormy weather by two mountains. Indeed, there are good reasons that Clark was both the home of the 13th Air Force and a former backup landing spot for the space shuttle.

In 2002, UPS faced a momentous decision. The Mainland and Hong Kong Closer Economic Partnership Agreement (CEPA) gave UPS the right to become wholly owned and end the joint venture with Sinotrans earlier than UPS had anticipated. While it could have waited another year or two, UPS didn't know if the financial circumstances would ever be better to pull the trigger.

When David Abney talks about the decision to become

wholly owned and start investing enormous UPS resources in China, it becomes clear that, to him, missing that opportunity would have been passing on the chance of a lifetime. "We took the view that this was our best shot at having our own operations in China," he says.

Richard Loi, UPS China's district manager as of late 2006, and his team started negotiating with Sinotrans in 2004 and eventually agreed on a $100 million buy-out fee, less than one-third of what FedEx eventually paid to get out of its Chinese joint venture. Prior to the operation being wholly owned, UPS China had 400 employees, and as of early 2007, there were 4,000 UPS China employees, a testament to the extraordinary effort by Loi and his managers to hire and train people even while running the business.

Today, UPS in China faces situations where in the past it could rely on its relationship with Sinotrans. For example, Steve Okun, UPS's head of public affairs in its Asia Pacific region, has found that getting central government approval in China for a UPS request actually just earns the company the right to go and try to get local approval.

But for the most part, every few months means new opportunities for UPS in China. Whether it's offering express package service across much of the country, opening UPS Supply Chain Solutions distribution centers, establishing driver incentive programs for getting customer leads, or opening UPS Express retail centers in Shanghai, UPS expects huge growth from its business in the world's most populous country.

OPERATING AROUND THE WORLD TODAY

The world is a big place with, as UPS has learned, many opportunities. In 2006, UPS International did $9 billion worth of business in a company with $47 billion in revenues. In the future, according to Abney, the percentage of international versus domestic revenue will only grow.

But the company must work to keep together a network of joint ventures, alliances, and contractors to create delivery operations in "non-Brown" countries. Along the way, UPS has learned how to be flexible and move fast to deal with various market conditions.

In India, for example, drivers from any company delivering goods from one state to another face bureaucratic obstacles more onerous than customs in Europe before the borders came down, with different taxes, different licenses, and different regulations. The antiquated Indian Postal Act of 1898, still on the books governing the country's mail system, is as good a metaphor as any for a country where delivering between different areas of the country is as difficult as delivering to another country.

To make this UPS world stay together, to mesh an entire international delivery system, takes a world-class IT system and UPS-tested processes, yes, but it also takes hundreds of thousands of UPS employees around the world who embrace the company's powerful culture. Eskew recalls how on one trip to China, he saw two delivery drivers standing at the rear of a package car on a busy downtown street. One driver raised the rear door of the vehicle, gestured to the packages piled to the ceiling, and along with the other driver, raised his arms in a definitive "hurrah."

"I think the international story is a tremendous story of our people finding the right way to be both consistent and flexible," says Kurt Kuehn, senior vice president of worldwide sales and marketing. "This is a story of how a company adapted to keep what is best about it, and still stayed relevant to its customers."

UPS RULES FOR THE ROAD

Creating a Truly Global Business

- **Export expertise, and culture, carefully.** American expatriates comprise less than one-tenth of 1 percent of UPS employees. The company understands that one size does not fit all, especially when expanding into global markets. Figuring out when to use expatriates and when to let go of the reins is one key to successfully operating overseas. Corporate cultural attributes can be woven into the local fabric over time.

- **Let the exceptions prove the rule.** UPS has ironclad ways of doing things, except when it doesn't. Despite its global brand and worldwide commitment to delivering packages on time, for example, *how* UPS achieves this in each country is largely up to that country.

- **Manage for the long haul.** Every company has growing pains, and companies that understand them as such have a better chance of riding out the rough patches. When UPS's international efforts still failed to turn a profit, most companies would not have tolerated the losses, but UPS stuck with its plan (while making necessary short-term adjustments) and its international service became the most profitable part of the business.

7

The Technology Company
That Delivers Packages

*"The information about a package is becoming as
important as the package itself."*

—Oz Nelson,

UPS CEO, 1990–1996

FOUR HOURS IN OREGON

Once each year, about a week or so before Christmas Day, a
trio of UPS Browntails lands at a tiny, nondescript airport in
Medford, Oregon, home of the high-end food distributor Harry &
David.

In the span of four hours or so, thousands of orders of Harry &
David fruit (the homegrown Royal Riviera Pears alone made the
company's name), candy, truffles, cheesecake, and other delec-
tables are loaded onto the three aircraft to begin their journey to
several strategically located, UPS–operated Harry & David distribution centers. Then, it's on to customers all over the world.

"For a few hours in this little town, it's like D-Day," says
Chuck Oeleis, UPS's client strategic account manager for Harry

& David. "One day there is basically an empty landing strip, the next day there are planes, trucks, and people loading hundreds of thousands of packages."

More than 90 percent of Harry & David orders made during the holidays reach customers within twenty-four hours, a percentage fairly unheard of in holiday shipping circles. Since using UPS, Harry & David has experienced far fewer customer service calls, product returns, and holiday revenue adjustments.

Before UPS technology enabled a complete shipping and tracking solution for Harry & David, the company had to painstakingly pore through shipping receipts to find this information, hours or even days after the fact.

Today, Harry & David's packages are tracked by using a UPS technology known as Quantum View. It allows Harry & David to see, via a secure Web site, an up-to-the-minute account of what it has shipped, who received it, the address at which it was received, and exactly when it was received. Harry & David doesn't need to contact UPS to get any of this information; UPS's groundbreaking package tracking technology, in essence, is Harry & David's groundbreaking package tracking technology. "There is a tremendous amount of information facilitated by UPS that is telling Harry & David about their shipments in real time," Oeleis says. Harry & David, like UPS, has learned to use technology as a strategic weapon to serve customers better.

With UPS's help, so has The Home Depot. With more than 2,000 stores, The Home Depot is the largest home improvement retailer in the world. With 2.5 billion page views annually and more than 30,000 products available online, its Web site, homedepot.com, receives more traffic than any other online destination in the home and garden category.

UPS and The Home Depot, two giants headquartered in Atlanta that try to work together on projects whenever they can, got together to find an inbound tracking solution for The Home Depot. The retailer wanted total transparency into the products coming in from thousands of suppliers, many of whom simply sent pallets full of goods when they were good and ready—not necessarily when The Home Depot was ready.

Just as The Home Depot wanted clarity into what it was receiving from its suppliers, so too, did The Home Depot's corporate customers want to see what The Home Depot was sending them. By using UPS's WorldShip technology, not only do The Home Depot's customers know which packages will arrive on which days, but they know what is in the package. For companies, inbound visibility is critical because it helps them balance inventory, plan customer promotions and incentives, and even schedule workers based on the workload. The Home Depot was also one of the first companies to use another UPS tool called CampusShip, which allows desktop UPS shipping within the sites of a self-contained corporate campus setting.

How does UPS make sure that its customer-focused technology works for customers like Harry & David and The Home Depot, and that its internal IT systems never go down? Welcome to Mahwah.

MIRACLE IN MAHWAH

UPS's world technology headquarters in Mahwah, a New York City bedroom community in northern New Jersey, keeps the company's global systems running 24/7, every day of the year.

Jim Medeiros, a trim man with a spring to his step that gets more pronounced as others grow more tired, is vice president for information systems shared services at UPS, which is a long-winded title for a job with a very clear task: "The sole reason for my existence," Medeiros says, "is to make sure our systems never go down. All of our Internet systems, all of our package systems, all of our airline systems, can never go down." Medeiros has instructed his staff that if anything significant does go amiss anywhere around the world overnight, he wants to know. Chief Information Officer Dave Barnes, who is based in Atlanta but keeps an office in Mahwah, hears about it one minute later.

Mahwah's nine IBM mainframes, and six more located in a data center near Atlanta called Windward, process twenty-seven million instructions a second, track fifteen million packages each day, coordinate the operations of an entire airline, collect and distribute package delivery data from 96,000 DIADs, and connect 149,000 work stations through 8,700 servers.

UPS owns the largest IBM relational database—its global package database—in the world. It's the biggest user of cellular phone minutes in the world. It's one of the biggest purchasers of PCs in the world. It employs 4,000 of its own software engineers, a number that leaves some Silicon Valley software executives taken aback. "Until 1988, UPS was basically run manually, with package data written down on paper," Medeiros says. "If the small number of computers we had were down for some reason, the reality was that we would still make our delivery commitments. Today, this whole place would stop, and that's just unacceptable."

Because the systems in Mahwah simply cannot fail, both the

bones of its underlying infrastructure and the mod-looking data center are backed up in an elegant architecture that the company labels "mirrored."

That means that there are two, or sometimes more, of every critical support system: two utility power feeds, seven generators, four unlimited power supply systems, two chilling plants cooling the computers and redundant data storage facilities. Even the innards of the main data storage devices have double panels in case the switches on one panel don't work.

Then, of course, there are two data centers: the Mahwah world headquarters and the slightly smaller Windward data center, with the six other IBM mainframes. The two share operating duties during the day, but if a meteorite took out the entire Mahwah facility, critical processes would be taken over in Windward, and vice versa. In Mahwah, the only thing there are not two of in the data center is janitors—and that's a precaution as well. For security reasons, only one cleaning person has access.

AN AFTERNOON WITH THE MAINFRAMES

While researching her definitive Harvard Business School case study on UPS's business transformation through technology, Dr. Jeanne Ross, a professor of computer science at MIT, visited Mahwah in 2000. Around the same time as the UPS site visit, she visited the data center of a New York investment bank. "At the bank, if you had asked one of the professional technicians to switch, say, that blue wire and that yellow wire, it would have taken them hours to find the right wires, the place was such a mess," Ross says. "In Mahwah, I felt like if I had been in the

CIO's office and he said, 'Hurry, switch the blue wire and the yellow wire,' I actually would have been able to do it, because the UPS design is very intuitive, and also very clean and labeled."

The spotless main room of the data center contains the nine IBM mainframe computers doing the heavy lifting of running a $47 billion company. Anyone who hasn't seen a mainframe computer in a few years can easily miss the 6' 6" computers that most resemble handsome entertainment centers.

Each mainframe occupies just two floor tiles by two tiles, or about twenty square feet. For comparison's sake, a UPS employee recently stepped off the number of tiles that UPS mainframes took up when the data center in Mahwah first opened in 1989. He stepped off twenty tiles by twenty, or about 400 square feet—twenty times bigger than the current model.

BACKUP SYSTEMS AT WORK

Today everyone at UPS IS can confidently say that the backup redundancies at Mahwah work exactly as planned. But prior to the summer of 2003 no one was really sure, because the system's mettle had never been seriously tested.

That all changed on August 14, 2003, the day that all of UPS's backup planning and redundant designs paid off. The massive blackout that plunged much of the eastern United States and Canada into total darkness left UPS executives counting on the backup generators in Mahwah to keep the powerful computers—and thus the company—up and running. When the blackout hit, no one knew exactly what would happen if it disabled Mahwah's mainframes. The six mainframes at the

Windward data center, running full-bore at 100 percent capacity, could theoretically handle the company's critical computing needs, but an additional glitch at that site would mean a company-wide, catastrophic failure.

Power outages, or power surges for that matter, can cripple a computer system. Any kind of fluctuation in power interrupts the processes of whatever operation the computer is performing; a full outage or surge can crash the system. So when Medeiros's office lights started flickering like a disco ball—his deputy operations manager Ed Zolcinski was meeting with him at the time—it was old-fashioned, bipedal power that propelled them down the hall, through the security checkpoints, and into the data center. Nothing was amiss—UPS's backup systems worked as planned.

The scale, infrastructure, and capacity at Mahwah are to a large extent responsible for powering UPS's technology transformation over the past two decades. Dr. Ross, the MIT professor, describes the information technology scene in the late 1980s and early 1990s this way: "A lot of companies at the time were just patching up and then waiting for the next part of their network to break down, and then patching that up," she says. UPS, on the other hand, built a broad infrastructure that could handle later add-ons.

Retrofitting a company of UPS's size to be a technology giant was incredibly painful and expensive, costing billions of dollars and forever changing the culture of the organization. But the economies UPS gained not only helped it leapfrog scores of competitors in the 1980s and 1990s, but made it into the 800-pound technology gorilla it is today. FedEx? "That's like comparing one hundred apples to ten bananas," says John Mazzella, an IBM executive who worked as the computer maker's account executive to UPS for more than ten years. "Different systems, and much different scale."

As an example of this difference in scale, the rise in packages processed daily by UPS during its 2006 peak season—fifteen to twenty-two million—was comparable to the total daily average volume at FedEx. "One of the things that analysts and our customers are staggered by is the scale here," Barnes says. "If you laid it all out, FedEx mostly has what we have from an IT standpoint. But ours just keeps going."

JIM CASEY: COMPUTER GEEK

Barnes has led IS at UPS since the retirement of Ken Lacy in February 2005. Lacy replaced the legendary Frank Erbrick in 1996, who had served as head of IS since 1984. Since its opening in 1989, the Mahwah facility has been affectionately known by some UPSers as The House That Frank Built, or alternatively among Erbrick's closest friends in UPS management, Frank's Pink Palace, a reference to the salmon-colored hue of the structure. "You have to remember, when Mahwah was built, UPS headquarters was a cement box in an office park in Greenwich," Erbrick says. "I think the scale here shocked a few people."

Many UPSers wouldn't guess it, but well before this trio of CIOs, one of the first computer geeks at UPS was grandfatherly company founder Jim Casey, who in photos is typically pictured next to package cars and in sorting hubs. He especially liked to talk about what computers could potentially do for UPS. There's an eyewitness.

Though he would never begrudge anyone that shared his love of computers, Leon Williams, a Mahwah software manager and the longest-tenured IS worker, with thirty-eight years at UPS as of late 2006, chuckles today at what passes for "computer literate." As a math major at Morehouse College in Atlanta in the mid-1960s, Williams started fiddling with *the one* computer on campus while working on class assignments.

"You know, it's not like you could buy software," Williams says. "Using a computer back then actually meant writing the code. You had to know computer coding just to get your program loaded." Today's laptops are about 100 times more powerful than the mainframes used when Williams first started writing programs.

Williams had a part-time UPS job at a hub in Atlanta, and as he neared graduation he heard that UPS was looking to expand its five-person National Systems and Computer Services (NSCS) group in New York. That group had gotten its start in 1964 when a man named Ray Gage founded it as a way to more efficiently process New York area CODs. Williams first had to pass a code-writing test, and soon enough he was one of thirteen new programmers in New York.

His first surprise was the jaw-dropping views of the Hudson River from the seventh floor of UPS's New York City hub on West 43rd Street and 12th Avenue, where the NSCS group sat one floor below the national corporate headquarters. Williams's second surprise was Casey's interest in computers. At that point, Casey was driven into work a few days a week from his apartment at the Waldorf-Astoria, and would sometimes visit with employees in the coffee shop, one of whom was Williams. Casey would ask the programmers what their backgrounds were, what kind of projects they were working on, and tell Williams and his colleagues how much the company needed them. "If he had lived another twenty years, I don't think you'd see a bigger champion of the computer at UPS than Jim Casey," Williams says. "He knew these things were going to transform the business."

Casey might have been prescient about computers, but that didn't mean that UPS was going to overly invest in them. Williams and his colleagues used a computer programming language known as Basic Assembly Language (BAL). What distinguished BAL was its reputation among programmers as a tight language, meaning the programmers used less code to make the commands. This also made it more challenging, because the code writer had to wring a lot of meaning out of very few lines of code. Given that the NSCS reported up through accounting at the time, it's not surprising that UPS wanted the computer programmers using BAL. "Computer memory was very expensive at the time," Williams says. "And UPS wanted us to use as little memory as possible."

FROM THE STONE AGE TO THE DIGITAL AGE

Nothing captures the UPS way of hanging back, hanging back, and hanging back until the very last moment—and then going full tilt once it decides on the correct path—like its technology transformation. Today, convinced that exploiting new technologies is the key to any future growth of the package delivery business, UPS routinely invests about $1 billion annually in customer-facing technology tools and internal technology processes, like the mainframes and data storage databases in Mahwah.

But it wasn't always that way. Though UPS had actually been an innovator in new technologies in its first decades, the company's enormous success in its middle decades, first as a retail delivery company and then as a common carrier, calcified management's desire to innovate from a technological point of view.

In fact, when UPS launched its IT revolution in the mid-1980s it wasn't anything that hundreds of companies of similar size and scope hadn't already contemplated. Historically, UPS had a reputation for innovation in industrial engineering, not systems.

While IE introduced some new technologies as it engineered hubs and package sorting facilities, those advances were based on mechanical engineering concepts rather than information technology. The time management studies in such areas as how drivers were to hang keys on their fingers or the optimum speed at which to walk 100 feet from a package car helped establish UPS as a great home for talented industrial and mechanical engineers.

Along with a reputation for innovation, industrial engineers at UPS were also known, at times, to cultivate personas as mad scientists. In Danbury, Connecticut, where an industrial engineering research operation was located for a number of years, staffers tested loading and unloading package cars with robots, only to find that the robots couldn't vary their movements enough under the available technology to be of any real use. It was an industrial engineer at UPS who came up with conveyor belts that could make turns. And Erbrick remembers the day he visited a Harrisburg, Pennsylvania hub for the grand unveiling of another UPS IE innovation: the custom drive-through car wash.

Erbrick and his colleague Bill Herlihy were standing on a hill, overlooking the facility like two proud generals at a battle.

They watched as the top of a package car was shaved neatly, completely off on the maiden run-through. "I was laughing so hard because I was thinking of how we were going to word the report," Erbrick says.

But there were far more successes for IE than gaffes, of course. Just the fact that the company could design processes to manually run a feeder network or a maintenance schedule for an entire airline stands as a Herculean achievement. "It's actually incredible that the company came as far as it did with virtually no automation," says Rino Bergonzi, the computer systems executive who Erbrick brought into UPS in 1984 to lead the development of UPS's computer systems. "The credit goes to IE, because they had these incredibly detailed processes for everything that kept the company competitive."

Computers, conversely, were thought of early on at UPS, as at most other companies, as useful primarily for data entry work. "They had a few computers for years before all of us techies got here in the early and mid-1980s," says John Nallin, who had been director of systems at Tenneco and came to UPS in 1987 as a systems manager and today is an IS vice president. "But it was just typing and printing out. There was no networking or connectivity."

So when were computers first introduced at UPS and why? And when did they really start to gain traction? Technology at UPS didn't begin with package tracking, though that's where most IS people at the company peg it to, because that was the first big, tangible IS achievement. It didn't start with the DIAD, either, and it certainly didn't begin with holiday shopping over UPS.com. It didn't even begin with the NSCS that started operating in New York in 1964.

A FOUNDATION FOR LATER INNOVATION

The computer age at UPS dawned in 1938 with the first IBM punch cards, or Hollerith cards, which were typically used by companies to group together pieces of data that would be laborious to sift through and group together manually. At some point in the 1960s, the business world began to notice that computers could speed the processes by which things got done, and UPS formed NSCS in 1964.

When Paramus, New Jersey, was established in the early 1970s as the central computer center, it marked the first separation of the IS operation from the rest of the business. Prior to that, the early computer initiatives had been centered in New York or one of the regional data processing groups that popped up in a few other cities.

Not surprisingly given the kind of work it did and its new location, IS developed its own culture at UPS. Even today in Mahwah, employees carry drinks around and drink coffee at their desks, something you wouldn't see at the corporate headquarters or out in the field, where UPS tradition dictates no food or drink in offices, hallways, or most conference rooms (the logic being that loaders and drivers aren't allowed to haul food and drink along with them on the job either, except during breaks).

Some of the early work that Williams and other programmers worked on was straight-on accounts payable, COD-type transactions. Williams remembers bags of thousands of COD cards coming in from other cities into New York to get entered into the system.

But a few early IS projects laid the foundation of some much later achievements, package flow among them. Early attempts at more efficiently moving packages from one place to another, in fact, date to the 1970s at UPS, marking the first significant partnership between those two distinct entities—the very established, accomplished IE group and the nascent IS group.

An IE team had been working on rudimentary tracking using a computer called the Radio Shack TRS 80, jokingly referred to as "Trash 80s" by the UPS industrial engineers. Writing programs in Fortran and Basic, the engineers' goal was to better manage the flow of packages and vehicular traffic out of the major hubs. They were attempting to build a database containing the historical records of which feeders went to which unloading dock upon arrival, and how long it took to unload the feeders once they were parked at the dock.

The idea was to compute the best unloading dock for each feeder to be directed to, depending on the size of the load, time of day, etc. In that way, a primitive way of balancing the flow of feeders, and thus packages, into a hub could be established. Williams and other IS professionals were pulled into the project to smooth out the engineers' coding, which tended to be brilliant solutions to the problem but sometimes missed coding steps or used redundant characters.

Appropriately enough, one of the first all-hands-on, groundbreaking computer projects at UPS was directly related to a customer need: proof-of-delivery. Much like today, businesses and individual consumers twenty, thirty, or forty years ago often wanted confirmation that a package reached its desired destination.

If a shipper called UPS to check on a shipment, the message would eventually reach a clerk, who had to go find the receipt signed by the receiver, which would have been filed somewhere in an administrative part of the hub. Then the clerk would take the signed receipt to the "tracing" department, made up mostly of women with extremely good handwriting.

A document called a "tracer" would then be created by the scribe, who would actually trace the signature onto a piece of vellum while holding the vellum paper over the signature on the receipt. The tracer document would then be mailed to the shipper. In all, it could take a week to receive confirmation. "If you were lucky, each person could do twenty or thirty of these tracers a day," says Nallin, whose group was in charge of automating this antiquated proof-of-delivery process.

If Nallin's group could get that package delivery information—a signature, bar code, or some other record of a confirmed delivery—onto a computer, anyone could just print out a confirmation, which could then be mailed to the shipper. The steps of physically filing the receipt, looking it up, and creating the tracer document could all be skipped. Nallin's group developed just such a tool, which eventually led to the creation of the DIAD. How? Seeing how much more quickly UPS could answer customer questions about packages in transit, the company reasoned that critical proof-of-delivery data—a tracking number, or perhaps the customer's signature itself—could automatically be entered into some kind of an electronic clipboard for drivers that would replace their traditional physical clipboards.

In addition, there would be loads of other useful data that would result from uploading that customer information: the exact times drivers made deliveries and real-time confirmation that a package was received. And, not to mention, drivers wouldn't have to worry about handwriting being misinterpreted, rain muddying up their entries, losing sheets of paper, and a host of other paper-related problems.

But enormous challenges complicated the development of an electronic clipboard for the UPS driver that could send and receive package data. For one, the appropriate electronic clipboard device had to be developed. Then, to do any real-time tracking information, the data had to be retrieved out of the electronic clipboard via some kind of terminal, and somehow sent back to a central repository of data. Third, even if UPS could achieve all this, there was still the cost of doing so. Any kind of system to track all packages—which numbered in the millions per day by the late 1980s—would be enormously expensive.

Besides, there were under 100 employees in the whole IS department as of 1984, and they were still doing mostly billing and clerical reports. UPS was so far behind other companies its size in using information technology that employees wondered if it could ever catch up. Other companies were already electronically collecting and sending package delivery data, namely FedEx, which had started doing business in 1972 and, according to a *New York Times* article, had spent almost $1 billion since 1980 on its tracking label technology to better trace packages.

When FedEx came up with its overnight express model, it didn't rest with that one idea. It started developing technology very focused on the customer. FedEx's devotion to the customer, for example, was also epitomized in its drivers' ability to pick up deliveries on the fly. Whereas UPS announced its scheduled pick-up timetables like an edict, FedEx came when the customer called, giving the drivers communications devices to receive and track orders. FedEx partnered with IBM to use a portion of the radio spectrum to transmit this data to and from the FedEx driver.

UPS, conversely, felt that customers benefited most from low rates that came from a cult-like focus on efficiency without bells and whistles or any deviation. Tracking for Next Day Air? You don't need that, UPS would say to the customer. Why pay for tracking when you know the package will arrive on schedule 98 percent of the time? Bulk discounts? Sorry, grannies in Pasadena have always gotten the same rates as Standard Oil and Republic Steel. Says Medeiros, the attitude was, "Hey, we're Big Brown, we tell you what's best, Mr. Customer." But Big Brown was overruled by John Q. Public when it came to package delivery tracking for express shipments. Customers wanted it, plain and simple. If not from UPS, then another company.

New competitors like Airborne Express, Emery Air Freight, and Purolator had jumped aggressively into the overnight business. By the end of 1984, at least eighteen companies offered overnight delivery services. Even the Postal Service was delivering overnight express.

In fairness to UPS, FedEx didn't even have a ground service at this point, so tracking its packages didn't offer the scale issues that UPS faced. FedEx's entire product portfolio was overnight express. Tracking millions of UPS's packages would be much different than tracking fewer than one million overnight packages going through just a few major air hubs. "When we were going to do it, we wanted a solution that could do all of our packages, though we knew we had to phase it in," says Nelson.

Simply, the company-wide feeling at UPS in the early 1980s, even with many competitors' technology structures evolving to be far more focused on the customer, was that its IE department had perfected manual package processing; why mess with it? Besides, business was good. In the domestic U.S. market, the company was happily transporting goods across state lines after decades of battles with state regulators. In 1984, in fact, UPS overtook the U.S. Postal Service Parcel Post business in the number of packages moved, 1.96 billion to 1.86 billion.

In other words, the picture was mixed. That things had to change was clear to some; not so clear to others. What UPS needed was one person to come up with a technology vision, convince others of its necessity, and then turn that vision into a reality. That person was Oz Nelson.

PLAYING CATCH-UP

Oz Nelson was an aberration as a UPS CEO because he didn't come up through operations or finance. His heart had always been in sales and marketing. Selling Big Brown internally on a technological revolution would be the biggest selling job of his career. In fact, even he didn't completely embrace the concept for some time. Nelson said to a *New York Times* reporter in the early 1980s about tracking packages that, "It's not to imply that these are not excellent services, but there is a definite cost to them. When you are in the package delivery business, you are in the pennies business. The trick is to get the pennies to add up to be profitable."

If being under the finance rubric had tended to give IS a low profile through the years, that placement was about to change the fortunes of the group forever. One day in the mid-1980s, CEO George Lamb, who had come up on the operations side of the business when Nelson had risen through sales, phoned Nelson and told him to come up to headquarters in Greenwich; Lamb had a proposition.

When he heard the idea, Nelson, who was leading sales and marketing at the time, couldn't have been more surprised. "I want you to be CFO," Lamb said, since the current CFO was leaving. Part of the reasoning was that Lamb trusted Nelson because of their work together getting UPS Next Day Air off the ground, so to speak. But Nelson was also being groomed for bigger things, and in appropriate UPS fashion, Lamb wanted him to understand more about the business than marketing and labor issues, which Nelson had also worked on.

Nelson had never spent a day in finance in his entire life. At the board meeting to discuss the appointment, directors asked Nelson what his qualifications were to be CFO, and he told them that his wife was an accountant. The reply? "Good, have her check your work."

As CFO, Nelson inherited the IS group. In 1984, the salesman in Nelson couldn't help but see the market share UPS was throwing away by not using the latest technology to serve its customers better. Amazingly, a year after UPS started its Next Day Air business, it had exceeded FedEx's profitability margin per package, due to the excellence of UPS's delivery processes. But given that success, Nelson kept pointing out just how UPS could soar out in front of the competition if it developed real-time data communication with drivers, package tracking, and the ability to do things like pre-load package cars more efficiently.

He approached Jack Rogers and explained that, as long as he had the computer group, he wanted to improve the group and see if UPS could not make some inroads on package tracking, as well as other issues. Soon enough, Rogers allowed Nelson to gather the best technological minds of the company and turn them loose to develop new ways for the company to use technology, both to support customer solutions and improve internal operations. Nelson formed a technology steering committee at the company, and he was careful to ask for the number two or three person in each UPS division to join the committee. He didn't want the leader of each division, as he was convinced that that's where the opposition to fundamental change would lie.

Nelson himself wasn't a techie; it would have been hard to find one in UPS outside of the ninety-person IS department at the time. But he started hiring hundreds of qualified information technology managers. Erbrick, the man Nelson plucked to turn around the company's IS infrastructure, was an unlikely technology missionary. Erbrick was out in California, as the controller of the Pacific region. A former feeder truck (not package car) driver and free spirit by UPS standards, Erbrick had already quit UPS in a pique at one point, and then returned to lead the Newark, New Jersey district, where he says he still holds the record for least productive district manager, where one year his district had ten work stoppages. "I think I retired that record," Erbrick says.

Much like the legitimate NSCS group in Paramus, Erbrick

used computers out in California to automate certain accounting processes, though seldom with approval. Very little of what Erbrick was doing was known by corporate headquarters back in Greenwich or the NSCS, so he actually hid some of his district's innovations. He had his staff write up a handwritten monthly report for Greenwich, even though his group had already automated the collating of the data. "Purchasing, payroll processing, all of that we did much more cheaply than the other regions because we were using computers to do the heavy lifting," Erbrick says. "I just didn't advertise how we did it."

A WATERSHED MEETING

During a fateful meeting with Rogers and Erbrick, Nelson forcefully presented his judgment that it was high time to start matching FedEx's technology by tracking overnight express packages as a start, and then expand to all ground deliveries as well. Nelson told Rogers that, according to UPS salespeople, corporate clients in particular wanted faster package tracking. Rogers asked Nelson how much it was going to cost, and Nelson answered about thirty-five cents per package. It was too much. "Give me six months," said Nelson, "and I'll have it down to ten cents." The compromise? Only overnight air packages would be tracked. It was a go.

The question was how this would happen. There were many different kinds of proposals, one of which was to simply outsource the company's entire computer operations. But ironically, it was an IE leader who helped keep the package tracking initiative, and thus IS, in-house. Future CEO Eskew, one of the company's leading engineers, argued successfully against the proposal to outsource all UPS computer operations. Outsourcing technology would have been a major departure from the way of keeping knowledge in-house and using self-reliance to solve problems. It took an industrial engineer, someone with clout, to preserve the UPS legacy of keeping important functions in-house, and labeling IS as one of those crucial functions.

Eskew, in fact, would come to personify the link between IE and IS. He grew into the business working on complex engineering issues, and he later morphed into a technologist. Eskew was a veteran of the group that would hash out the technology roadmap for the company. As a member of Nelson's technology steering committee, he helped formulate the stategy related to UPS.com. And in the mid-1990s, Eskew was one of the first UPS executives to spot the Internet's potential to streamline operations, develop new products, and increase sales.

Erbrick told his top IS managers that there was one priority when it came to package tracking and everything that came with it: speed. "I told everyone, 'I don't care what it costs, as long as it happens fast,'" Erbrick says.

Erbrick went on a hiring binge, snapping up hundreds of talented programmers and software engineers. Pat Brady, who works in Mahwah today, was in charge of human resources in the Paramus technology center then. "It was unbelievable, every week you'd see hundreds of new people coming through," Brady says. "It was very un-UPS-like. And a lot of employees were thinking, who are all these people?"

Dave Barnes was recruited by Erbrick in 1984 to serve on his IS team after stints both as an accountant and head of data processing at UPS in St. Louis. Over the next twenty years, he would lead a number of technology projects, from helping to bring the UPS brokerage group into the computer age, to rolling out various international IS advances, to organizing the business side of IS as financial systems coordinator.

AN INNOVATION OVERSEAS

Besides current CIO Barnes, one of the folks Erbrick brought into the company during this massive recruiting push was Medeiros, who in 1988 found himself as a UPS project manager in its international division, working on a project in Germany. That team developed a customs clearance solution that moved goods across European borders much more quickly, working with UPS computer engineers to develop the package tracking innovation that later became known as smart scanning.

In the late 1980s, UPS was pushing hard to gain a bigger international presence. DHL had far more name recognition and market share. In the same way that a booming ground business in the United States didn't create the urgency needed for UPS to take on risky technology projects, the company's relative lack of presence in Europe made just those kinds of endeavors feasible.

In UPS's international operations, Canadian and German customs officers greatly slowed down business by choosing a great many packages randomly, removing the labels, and opening the package to see if they contained goods that were not allowed into the country. It could take anywhere from twenty-four to forty-eight hours for a UPS package to clear customs. Eventually, UPS decided to find a way to help customs agents do their jobs better. But the technology didn't exist.

Medeiros's group, working with information technology consultants from Arthur Andersen, developed a system that collated information about the packages and sent the data on to customs a day or two before the parcels arrived, giving the agents much better and earlier information about which packages should be held up and examined. What resulted was an entire class of UPS packages that gained automatic clearance, greatly increasing profit margins. "The fact that our international operations actually drove the smart scanning sometimes gets lost," Medeiros says.

As *BusinessWeek* said in an article at the time: "UPS has designed a system that codes and tracks packages, automatically billing customers for customs duties and taxes." Soon, the technology was being used back in the States to begin the years-long march to creating the "smart package," a huge step in the march toward full package tracking. "Our innovations tracking packages overseas was sort of a confirmation that we were on the right path domestically, that this was the way to go," Bergonzi says.

The achievement wasn't without its challenges. At one meeting in London, the IS leaders of several European countries told Medeiros that they had their own ways of tracking packages, their own ways of doing accounts payable, and their own ways of backing up critical data. Medeiros went back to Greenwich and told CIO Erbrick that several country managers didn't want the new system. Erbick wasn't happy about it, but with a company growing as fast as UPS was, good ideas were bound to come from all sorts of nooks and crannies around the organization.

THE DIAD STORY

Initially, a critical piece of the package tracking system failed. The DIAD was remarkable technology, featuring the ability to electronically capture signatures on a scale never before contemplated. However, when the DIAD was rolled out on a very limited basis in 1989, it experienced durability, performance, and reliability problems. Drivers longed to return to their trusty clipboards and paper receipts, damn the inconvenient smudges during rainstorms. Billed as a collaboration between IE and IS, the DIAD initiative needed help if it was going to succeed, and the clear leader at the time of marrying wireless data transmission with mobile hand-held terminals was Motorola.

The leader of the project at Motorola was Elisha Yanay, the head of Motorola Israel. One of the problems with the design of the original DIAD was that UPS had not decided which communications platform to rely on to transmit data. UPS was looking at radio communication, the technology FedEx used for its package tracking, as well as cellular communications. Motorola Israel and UPS solved this issue with two different, slightly tweaked versions of the DIAD, one that relied on radio technology and one based on cellular communication.

The new DIADs were a hit in the field. The same drivers who

had been bitterly complaining about having to use the new tool asked district managers why it had taken so long to get one.

Clearly, choosing good vendors, including IBM, Motorola, Andersen Consulting, and McKinsey, was a key to UPS's technological achievements in the late 1980s and early 1990s. "We brought a lot of the expertise in," Bergonzi says. "For a lot of things, you don't want to buy expertise if you can rent it."

DON'T TOUCH THAT DIAL

A bigger decision than who would design and build the DIAD was the method of transmitting the package data. There were obstacles to both potential solutions. To use radio technology, UPS would have to apply for and purchase a portion of the radio spectrum, no major piece of which was available commercially at the time. As far as building a cellular network that could cover the area UPS needed—the entire contiguous forty-eight states—well, that had never even been attempted.

The smart money would have been on radio technology. All the plans were in place to build what would be a nationwide radio frequency over which UPS could send and receive network data. When people think of radio communications, they think of their morning traffic report. But radio frequencies can also carry radio data instead of voice data, according to Doug Fields, who coordinated the project for UPS.

The question was just how UPS would get allocated its own national frequency. The frequencies used for purposes such as commercial broadcasting, taxi company operations, and walkie-talkies had long since been saturated. UPS settled on a plan in which it could take over the 220 MHz spectrum for commercial use, and open up some portion of it to the public domain as a charitable act. The 220 MHz spot on the dial was being used by the military, police officials, and approved organizations like ham radio clubs.

First, UPS had to gain FCC approval to get the dial space. Then it had to build transmitting towers close to its large-volume metropolitan areas, which would be no easy feat. After all, how much spare room for towers was there in New York?

All sorts of groups tried to exploit UPS's desire to secure a portion of the FCC spectrum. Because small bits of the spectrum were given out in a lottery to purchasers each year, UPS was inundated with dubious offers to purchase pieces of the spectrum. "I had a consortium of dentists who called me a bunch of times offering to sell me their piece of the spectrum," says Fields. "It was well known that we were in the market for the 220."

While UPS was waiting for the FCC, as well as facing a hugely expensive job of putting in the infrastructure and then building the radio base, it purchased II Morrow, a company that made the hardware for two-way radio data communications. Everything was in place.

About the time that UPS was fully committed to the radio spectrum solution, in the mid-1980s, cell phone technology took off. Thousands of businesses subscribed seemingly overnight to cell service. Erbrick wanted to leave nothing at the negotiating table. A young IS employee on Doug Fields's staff, Mark Dodge, volunteered to take an in-depth look at the cellular options, and Erbrick assented, although he thought it was a "bunch of bunk."

John Nallin described a meeting with Fields and Dodge,

when Fields hauled out a map of the U.S. "He took this map that showed hundreds of cell carriers and where they had coverage," Nallin says. "And he said to me, 'Give us a shot.'"

It was a rather brash goal. Did UPS—still a technology neophyte in many ways—think it could actually build the first ever nationwide cellular network? Could UPS sell an entire industry on such collaboration?

If nothing else, Erbrick and Nallin thought they might be able to use Fields's and Dodge's research as leverage against the FCC. Perhaps if Dodge dug up some useful cellular pricing data, the thinking went, Erbrick could use the cellular threat to put some heat on the FCC to make a decision.

Then a funny thing happened. Someone forgot to tell Dodge that his mission was doomed. It turned out that the prospect of building the first ever national cellular network for a market-leading, brand name company like UPS was a challenge more than a few cell companies were more than happy to accept. Craig McCaw, the cell phone pioneer and founder of McCaw Communications, was the most enthusiastic. With McCaw acting as the lead negotiator with his fellow cell phone carriers, a unique contractual arrangement was forged with about forty companies.

UPS was able to obtain nationwide coverage at a fixed price well below the sixty cents per minute that was typical of the time. The cell phone companies, for their part, could still run their usual traffic over their respective portions of the national network.

Most significant was that UPS didn't have to own any of the network. It belonged to the Baby Bells and other cell phone companies that McCaw had recruited to form the consortium, and UPS's data was just along for the ride. The deal also reflected the entire approach of Nelson and Erbrick to building UPS's technology infrastructure. "Frank never wanted to build just to build," says John Mazzella of IBM. "He'd say, 'Why build the technology when someone else has already built it?' "

In the end, the consortium swelled to more than 100 cell carriers banded together to blanket the entire country and create a communications network that carried data to and from UPS package cars.

FIRING ON ALL CYLINDERS

With the cellular network in place, the system was in full sync. Before 1989, remember, UPS was recording package data on eight to nine million packages a day pretty much the way Bob Cratchit from Dickens's *A Christmas Carol* wrote up the ledgers for Scrooge. By 1992, UPS package tracking technology was the best in the business, handling far more transactions every day than FedEx. In 1993, UPS introduced its innovative Total-Track, the first nationwide cellular mobile data system, which instantly provided customers with tracking information for all air and ground packages. On the day the package tracking system became fully deployed, Erbrick rang the famous bell at UPS headquarters, the same one that had been rung on the day that UPS completed the Golden Link, as well as other milestone accomplishments.

Another critical research and development milestone was a

mid-1990s initiative called the customer automation system. UPS essentially asked its customers to provide them with more data at the time of shipping, the better to create smart packages that would go through the sorting system faster. UPS packages with a smart label essentially instruct the sorting equipment what to do with them.

That initiative evolved into WorldShip, a software application supplied free of charge to UPS corporate clients, who then use it to track their shipments to customers. To date, there have been more than 600,000 customer installments of WorldShip, which is comparable to the numbers that software companies in Silicon Valley typically install for a well-received product.

Current CIO Barnes notes that today, through WorldShip and other tools, the package information on 95 percent of UPS's average daily volume is electronically transmitted to UPS by the customer. That's how UPS can process more than fifteen million packages per day.

One of UPS's strategies in the late 1990s was to become the preferred vendor for major Internet retailers like Amazon.com. UPS.com was set up in the Innoplex, a 230,000 square-foot dot.com-ish tech facility based in a former Alpharetta, Georgia, furniture plant. The Innoplex was as close to a dot.com as UPS would ever come, and the idea was to develop Web-based applications like UPS Online Dossier and UPS Online Courier. Online Courier securely delivered documents via e-mail, while Online Dossier took security to another level through online digital certificates. By 2001, it was estimated that UPS was delivering more than half of all items ordered online in the United States.

THE FUTURE OF TECHNOLOGY AT UPS

Twenty years ago, UPS threw caution to the wind and spent whatever it had to catch up and pass the competition. Today, it thinks its technology is up to the task. Is it?

In a speech Erbrick gave in 1989, he laid out the dire consequences of standing still in information technology, saying that "information systems are critical to the existence of the company, and failure to address our needs in this field could result in disaster for us all . . ."

What would Erbrick do today with UPS's technology, which has improved every year but hasn't gotten a full-scale overhaul since he left? For example, though there is one global package database, there is still no single UPS customer database.

"I'd throw everything in the air again and see where it landed," Erbrick says. He doesn't mention FedEx as a competitor for the twenty-first century but Citigroup, Microsoft, and anyone else that can manage information. The key technology questions that UPS faces are which technologies will be important for the next ten years, and how should UPS leverage these technologies to stay ahead of the competition?

Are the answers the customer database? Aligning the Supply Chain Solutions systems with small package systems, which are somewhat separate right now? What about finding ways to extract more value out of the current package database, something Erbrick suggests? Or how about a point made by Kurt Kuehn, that new technological advances at UPS will likely be more focused on the recipient, not the sender, of packages?

The continuing role of technology at UPS is one of the issues that the strategy group, headed by Vern Higberg, has been considering. One thing is for sure: UPS has the infrastructure and the cash to make the changes it needs. From those five employees when Leon Williams came to work on the seventh floor of the UPS New York building on West 43rd Street, there are now 4,700 technology workers at UPS—hardware developers, hardware engineers, software engineers, systems developers. It's interesting to think how many will be there five years from now, as UPS continues to be one of the most successful technology—yes, that's technology—companies in the world.

UPS RULES FOR THE ROAD

The Technology Company That
Delivers Packages

- **When forming a task force, look past the top.** When former CEO Oz Nelson formed a technology steering committee, he chose the number two- or three-ranked employee in each division. Nelson's theory was that any opposition to change would likely come from the very top of a business unit.

- **Embrace a brave new world**. Exploiting new technologies is the key to future growth in the package delivery business and probably yours, as well. UPS annually invests $1 billion in technology—not for technology's sake—but to support its business strategy.

- **Technology creates better customer service**. Technology is not only beneficial to improving a company's internal operations, it is also a key component of a service culture. The end product of UPS's technology focus is its ability to serve its customers better—so they in turn can serve *their* customers better.

8

The Ownership Company

"I could always see a challenge and opportunity in our
organization and never thought of leaving."

—HAROLD OBERKOTTER,
UPS CEO, 1973–1980

TRAINING DAY

Abby Nathisuwan summoned the courage to confront her supervisor. "They want a report on every package, every day,
even the exceptions," she said of a very demanding UPS
customer. "Where the packages went, what time they went.
They call all the time and want more detail. Now you want
me to take on more customers. If I have one more, I am literally going to go crazy; do you understand? I can't take it anymore."

The young Korean supervisor seemed to empathize, and
clearly wanted to help. But he didn't know what to say; this
woman was at the end of her rope.

"Don't you understand, it's just too much for me to deal
with," she reiterated. "I can't send out whole reports to

customers every day when they can easily track the packages themselves."

"Yes, I understand," came the shell-shocked reply. Then silence in the room. But, after a few seconds, a recovery. "Are you asking to change jobs?" he said. "Or do you have something else in mind?"

Jerry Cass, sitting just outside the small knot of five or six observers, leapt up from his chair. "That's exactly right," he said, pleased that the struggling supervisor had found a way to mollify the employee. "First find out what she wants. Is she just looking to vent a little, does she need more help, or does she not want to do that job anymore?"

It was time for Cass and his trainees to wrap up the role-play exercise and join the rest of the twenty-four recently minted UPS Asia Pacific region supervisors from China, Japan, Malaysia, Taiwan, Thailand, and Korea, among other countries. Soon, Asia Pacific region president Ken Torok would be dropping by to address the Supervisor Leadership School (SLS), a training summit being held at a Singapore hotel to hone the leadership skills of UPS Asia's brightest young employees.

Cass, a thirty-year veteran of UPS who spent the early part of his career in operations before turning to in-house training full-time, was ecstatic with the improvement shown over the course of several role-playing scenarios (if there is one universal about training, according to Cass, it's that everyone dreads role playing, at first). "You think *you* don't like role-play exercises," Cass later says to a visitor. "Try doing it in your second, or sometimes third, language, like these folks have to."

According to Nathisuwan, who manages six employees in a

UPS customer call center in Bangkok, Thailand, she wasn't really acting. "That was a real story, a real issue that I had with someone who reported to me," she would later say. "People have their limitations, and every day as a UPS supervisor you have to face something different."

For Nathisuwan and her twenty-three colleagues, this eleven-day training session at the SLS in the early summer of 2006 is their first real taste of recognition on a regional level. They've been selected based on performance, yes, but also based on their potential to be future leaders at the company. For most of them, it's also their first exposure to Asia Pacific president Torok and other regional leaders. And for some, it's also their introduction to UPS outside of their own country, to a world apart from their everyday call center, industrial engineering department, or package sorting hub.

"This is by far the best training I've ever had," Nathisuwan says. "I have the benefit of learning from a company that's spent ninety-nine years getting everything right. Being a new supervisor is a very hard job, and I need some guidelines and techniques to do it, and UPS is giving them to me."

Cass has managed UPS seminars and training modules all over the world, taught seasoned executives and new employees, Americans and Armenians, managers and supervisors. Supervisors, the first level of UPS management, are his favorite group, especially when it comes to international locations. "Managers and directors, their English is usually rusty, and they are not as open to new ideas," Cass says.

It's up to him, the lone American of three instructors at this particular SLS, and his fellow trainers to make sure that these potential UPS executives leave with a deeper "toolkit" than when they arrived. But the goal of this leadership meeting is at least as cultural as it is skill-based.

The UPS emphasis on teamwork, a willingness to readily switch jobs or even career goals, an acceptance that being in management means picking up and moving every few years, the taboo against openly politicking to get one's way, the ability to think long-term and not be consumed by immediate needs—these core values didn't blossom by accident, and are likely quite foreign to the cultural norms in many Asian countries.

If they are not introduced to young managers in the fastest growing segments of UPS's market—such as China and her neighbors—those values will never take hold. So, Cass's job is really to ensure that these new supervisors have bought into UPS, into being "owners" of the company, even if they don't own a single share of stock, though most do already.

The chain of imparting "ownership" doesn't end there, of course. The supervisors then must hand it down to their team, in the same way that generations of UPS drivers and package loaders have been entrusted with that sense of ownership. It's telling that in West Germany in the mid-1970s, UPS's operation foundered partly because driver jobs were regarded as undesirable, low-status positions. A generation later, UPS drivers in Germany and the rest of Europe have that same ownership and pride that U.S. drivers do.

"This training will definitely help me train my people better," says Kuohsien Huang, another SLS participant. Huang is a Taiwan native who graduated from the University of Maryland and works in Japan as an industrial engineering supervisor. In Japan, Huang has both retention and morale problems, because, like

West Germany in the mid-1970s, it's hard to recruit people for UPS in Japan.

For one thing, there's essentially no such thing as a working college student or a college graduate who chooses to deliver packages. "If you are at UPS in Japan, it means that you are not in college and you probably didn't go to college," Huang says. UPS in Japan has recently seen some success in building its sales force, which has doubled after the recent dissolution of UPS's joint venture there. "There are a ton of new people, and a lot of them don't know much about UPS yet; there is some confusion in the market about UPS and Yamato after the end of the joint venture."

Speaking of joint ventures, that model for UPS entering countries in Asia has left some residual confusion and conflict in the effort to get employees to take ownership of their jobs the UPS way. In China with former joint venture partner Sinotrans and in Japan with Yamato, many employees were brought into the wholly owned UPS operation from the legacy company because UPS needed to grow so fast.

"Integrating everyone into one company and having them all identify with UPS is a challenge," says Richard Loi, district manager of China. Sinotrans employees, for example, were not used to UPS's rigorous performance standards and high levels of customer service. "But as we continue to hire more people and train them completely on UPS standards, you'll see more of a connection between UPS China and some of the more mature UPS operations," Loi says.

One of the most mature UPS operations in Asia is Hong Kong. Charlotte Or, a UPS accountant attending SLS, worked in Hong Kong from 2000 to 2004. She moved to Beijing when UPS was in the midst of its push to establish wholly owned operations in China. Or says that the sense of belonging at UPS Hong Kong was very developed, and that professionals there felt much attached to the American company. "We all knew who Jim Casey was, that sort of thing," Or says. "We knew that UPS history was very important to the company."

In Beijing, starting in 2004, it was up to Or and her supervisor to build the accounting department from three accountants to fifty, and help imbue the new hires with the same sense of UPS ownership that she had. Some of these new hires came from Sinotrans. "After we went 'Brown,' we had so many new people who were not familiar with UPS procedures and ways of doing things, and in China there is no history of corporate training," she says. "At Sinotrans, for example, training didn't exist, so we had to systematically start from the beginning with everything about the job, and UPS."

Now, in the span of two years, she has been promoted from assistant supervisor to supervisor to finance manager. "The best part of working for UPS is the opportunity," Or says. "What we try to tell everyone is that they can't get promoted until they plan for their own successor. That's the way the company stays strong."

With such accomplished young professionals as Nathisuwan, Huang, and Or at SLS, it seems overkill that Cass has bedecked the conference room with posters reminding trainees of UPS's role in the world ("Our Purpose: We Enable Global Commerce"), and the importance of working together to achieve a common goal ("Dream Team: Diversity, Reliability, Effectiveness, Adaptability, Model Communicator"). But it was typical UPS: leave nothing to chance.

After Ken Torok arrived and spent thirty minutes reviewing UPS history with the employees, he opened the session up to questions. One young man in the group asked if it was possible that one of the attendees at that day's meeting could ever become the CEO of UPS, or if that post would forever go to an American. Torok answered that how far anyone went in UPS was up to that individual, that there were no limits, but that everyone at SLS should remember one thing: "It doesn't matter how successful you are at UPS. Our customers always like the drivers best." Now, that's a real dose of UPS culture.

A CULTURE OF OWNERSHIP

Not all of UPS's 427,000 worldwide employees are technically "owners," and since the company became publicly traded in November 1999, about two-thirds of stock ownership resides outside the company. Today's UPS district and regional managers, drivers, package sorters, airline pilots and mechanics, industrial engineers, software developers, security officers, marketing and sales professionals are entitled to that same sense of ownership and partnership that UPSers have enjoyed since 1927.

That doesn't mean that all employee incentives are completely aligned or that they pursue the same exact rewards. For example, as part of their compensation packages, managers and supervisors receive stock awards based on company performance, while hourly employees must purchase stock, albeit at a 10 percent discount to the market.

The idea of employee ownership, however, goes well beyond

possession of UPS stock. It's the singular UPS cultural brew of stick-to-it-iveness, self-interest, and shared identity that leads such an incredibly diverse group of individuals to seek common cause. The company has built an incredibly positive culture by emphasizing a highly democratic human resources recipe, one that virtually no other major global company has attempted. Lea Soupata, recently retired senior vice president of human resources and former member of the UPS board of directors, credits UPS's promote-from-within credo as the glue that ties everyone to the company, even if an employee doesn't own a single share of stock.

Whereas nearly every company in the Fortune 500 talks the talk about finding the best and brightest people, UPS has figured out better than most how to both painstakingly nurture employees and consistently challenge them to perform better. The dual results of this philosophy are very low recruiting and retention costs and an incredibly loyal workforce. UPS reports a minuscule 8 percent turnover rate among full-time managers worldwide, including retirements. During the run-up to Y2K, when programmers were jumping from company to company getting the most money they could and companies were forced to offer "stay" bonuses, UPS did nothing of the sort. About 10 percent of UPS's programmers left that year, far lower than the industry standard.

For UPS drivers, the turnover rate is even lower than managers, about 5 percent, including retirements. After the initial equity offering in 1927, drivers couldn't acquire UPS stock again until 1995, yet the concept of ownership was still handed down to hourly employees from previous generations. Indeed, one didn't need stock to realize—Teamsters' traditional hard-nosed negotiating notwithstanding—UPS offered the best working conditions, chance of advancement, salary, and customer base for someone who drove for a living.

Jim Casey figured out seventy-five years ago that employees *want* to leave their respective comfort zones, and that the best way to successfully promote in-house was to hand managers just enough responsibility so that people were almost in over their heads. New drivers dispensed hundreds of packages with no one watching over their shoulders. Young managers were sent across the country to open hubs. Successful industrial engineers learned that their next position would be on the finance side of the business.

Subsequently, an army of managers developed under Casey with incredible operational, financial, and geographic experience. A sense of ownership proliferated as managers began to understand the whole company, to realize the operational challenges in different cities (New York City having always been a unique environment, because of its density) and in the various operational nooks and crannies within the company.

And that's still how the company is managed today. Rocky Romanella, a UPS region manager, remembers the day he was told the next stop for him and his family was Iowa. Romanella, a native New Yorker born in Little Italy, recalls that even as he knew the move would eventually help his professional advancement, he was thankful that at least he had four children who might enjoy Iowa. "If I hadn't had kids, relocating to Iowa might have been tough," Romanella says. "But you know when you become a supervisor, when you accept that level of responsibility for the company, part of the deal is going on the road."

Another key to the ownership company is that most UPS middle managers and senior managers started as drivers or part-time package handlers. When even the top managers of a company start at the bottom, it not only enables them to understand where the real work gets done but it gives every employee the incentive to, as Casey would have put it, "saw wood." "How many Fortune 100 companies have had all their CEOs start pretty much at the bottom of that very company?" says former UPS public relations director Joe Tranfo.

When Benn Konsynski first worked as an adviser to UPS more than a decade ago, he thought he knew what he was getting into: advising a staid old company that delivered packages and employed tens of thousands of truckers. "I really thought I would be dealing with a bunch of ex-Teamsters," says Konsynski, a management professor at Emory University in Atlanta. "But instead, you have these bright energetic people. I have worked with many of the largest and most advanced companies. I have never worked with a more intelligent, creative, and committed management team. One secret was the college kids that started with good-paying jobs that turned them into lifelong career commitments."

One idea that Konsynski posits is that the sense of continuity and ownership is so strong in UPS because employees understand that it's not just their current job that they "own." Konsynski says that, generally, employees are far more likely to cooperate with someone with whom they could very well be working closely in a year or two, or whose job they might even eventually wind up with.

From the very birth of the company, Casey nurtured an expansive, inclusive sense of ownership. That same sense of ownership that Charlotte Or showed in helping to build the UPS China accounting department made it possible for UPS China to expand from 400 employees to 2,500 in a nine-month period in 2005, when UPS jumped to a one-year head start in becoming a wholly owned business in China.

Managers-owners, owners-managers. Even after the company has been public for almost a decade, it's still sometimes hard to tell the difference.

AUGUST 1997

It was perhaps the very success of its relationship with employees over the previous ninety years that made the events of August 1997 so painful for UPS. The company that would conclude the decade with one of the biggest and most successful IPOs in history first had to weather its only nationwide strike.

The great irony of the fifteen-day strike, which lasted from shortly after midnight, August 4 through August 20, 1997, was that CEO Jim Kelly had successfully served as UPS's national labor manager for several years. As CEO from 1990 through 1996, Oz Nelson relied heavily on Kelly to negotiate with the Teamsters. Nelson says that Kelly was the best-prepared CEO UPS had ever had up to that point, and certainly the one most well-prepared to deal with the union.

Jeff Sonnenfeld, a Yale management professor who while at Harvard spent a year working with UPS, pays Kelly the highest compliment a UPSer could ever hope for. "What you often heard about Jim Kelly was that he was the quintessential Jim Casey manager," Sonnenfeld says. "He could talk to guys on the loading dock as easily as he could talk to an Internet geek; a very sophisticated guy who was personally unassuming."

In fact, under Kelly and labor negotiator predecessors like Dan McKnight and Joe Tranfo, UPS had worked with the Teamsters to forge new breakthroughs in labor relations. The Teamsters had always understood that UPS was critical to the health of its union due to its sheer size. Since UPS's first contract with the union in 1939, UPS had worked with Teamsters leaders to hammer out agreements that made the UPS Teamsters well paid compared to most Teamsters drivers, but insisted on flexibilities that UPS needed, such as moving UPS trailers via rail rather than ground over long distances, allowing the hiring of part-time drivers to deliver express packages for better competitiveness, assisting other drivers if a delivery run was completed early, or accepting a cut in hours if there wasn't enough work.

Another reason for the good working relationship between UPS management and the Teamsters through the years was that most members of the management team had, in fact, been Teamsters. To this day, every UPS CEO started in the trenches of the company, and that certainly was the case for management in 1997 as well. They understood what it was like to spend the day on a loading dock, drive in snow, lift seventy-pound packages, and make sure that every single package was delivered. In short, management knew the difference between a job at headquarters and a job in the field, and the union had always respected that. Eskew, for example, is fond of saying that the gleaming UPS corporate office in suburban Atlanta is not really UPS. "The real UPS is out in the hubs, out in the districts," he says.

The truth was that for many years, in an echo of the old line about General Motors and the country, what was good for UPS was often good for the Teamsters. For example, when UPS expanded into the common carrier business on a large scale in the mid-1950s, then-Teamsters president Jimmy Hoffa was concerned about the number of part-time jobs, as opposed to full-time jobs, being created.

McKnight, then UPS's chief labor negotiator, met with Hoffa about it. McKnight looked across the table and said, "Look Jim, we have the opportunity to go into a business that will add thousands of jobs to the Teamster payrolls. Right now, those are Postal Service jobs, and they could be Teamster jobs." Hoffa, as was his wont when provided with new information that might change his mind, looked at McKnight and wordlessly went on to the next subject. Later the word came back to UPS: Jimmy gives his okay.

Kelly got his first taste of a grueling negotiation during the thirteen-week Eastern Conference of Teamsters strike in 1976. For more than three months, no one could ship to the East Coast between Maine and North Carolina via UPS as Tranfo and Kelly negotiated day after day with the Teamsters Eastern Conference leadership. "Jim was with me during that strike and I think that kind of experience helped him later on, because he saw how the company supported us the whole time," Tranfo says. "He really became someone who could deal with any of the local unions."

THE NEGOTIATIONS

Partly due to Kelly's hard-won experience in working with the Teamsters, the mood in Atlanta among the UPS management team was one of cautious optimism entering the summer of 1997. But there were some troubling signs as the August 1 deadline crept closer.

Several offers from UPS chief negotiator Dave Murray to the Teamsters hadn't been replied to, even while Teamsters president Ron Carey was telling the press that UPS was not serious about negotiating. Nelson, now retired, ran into Carey at the Downtown Athletic Club in New York City and made a point about how contentious the Teamsters' rhetoric had already gotten.

Nelson asked Carey if he really wanted to push UPS toward concessions that would put the company's long-term stability in question. UPS had more Teamsters on the payroll than any other company, Nelson reminded Carey. Couldn't they maintain that model of a jointly successful union and company that their predecessors had worked so hard to achieve? "They already had higher wages and benefits at UPS than at any other Teamsters company," Nelson says. Carey told Nelson he had made some good points and that they should talk again. "He never called me back," Nelson says.

The other red flag for UPS was that not only was Carey up for re-election, he was also being investigated for diverting Teamster funds into his own campaign war chest. It didn't matter who headed the Teamsters—Hoffa or other Carey predecessors like Dave Beck, Roy Williams, or Jackie Presser—internal politics within the union often made for highly charged rhetoric at the negotiating table. "Negotiations, generally, go down to the wire with the Teamsters," Kelly says. "The problem in that particular case was that it seemed that everything had been orchestrated and planned before negotiations began."

Of the twelve-member Teamster negotiating team, only Carey

and one other person had actually been a UPS driver or package loader. The rest were policy experts, labor lawyers, and professional negotiators. That contrasted with UPS's negotiating team, which was filled with former UPS Teamsters, since UPS managers almost always work their way up to their positions. That dynamic created the astonishing situation of a group of former Teamsters being lectured by mostly non-Teamsters about how bad life was for current Teamsters. "It wasn't even a close call about which side had the common touch, so to speak," says Yale's Sonnenfeld.

The Teamsters negotiators trumpeted two main issues: part-time workers and pensions. The number of full-time versus the number of part-time jobs had always been a sticking point between the union and UPS. But there have always been very good reasons for the part-time positions at UPS.

To meet time commitments, packages have to stay in almost constant motion. They can't be warehoused or stored until there are a certain number to process. Instead they are handled in short bursts of time, between three to five hours in the middle of the night to meet delivery times the next day, and between three and four hours to load vehicles in the mornings for the day's committed deliveries. So in most locations where packages are sorted and processed, there simply isn't eight hours of work available.

Also, many UPS employees are drawn to part-time work, either because they can hold another job at the same time, as some teachers and clergy do, or so they can go to school, such as those UPS employees who attend Metropolitan (Metro) College in Louisville, Kentucky. Metro College is a collaboration between UPS, the state of Kentucky, University of Louisville, and two community colleges, with tuition paid by UPS and Kentucky. A closely related point about UPS's part-time culture is often overlooked: It serves as an excellent port of entry for future managers. Many talented employees today at UPS could have had their pick of jobs after college, but were attracted by the UPS culture and teamwork after they were exposed to it as a student part-timer.

But this time around, things were different. The Teamsters claimed the moral high ground early in the debate with the part-time issue. Carey accused UPS of making a billion dollars in profits, while at the same time cutting back on the number of full-time job opportunities and keeping thousands of people who worked thirty-five hours a week classified as part-timers.

Carey had very skillfully found a flash point with the public. Much like recent fears of outsourcing, there was a concern in the mid- and late-1990s that companies were too often shifting previously full-time work to contractors and part-timers to avoid paying a full range of benefits. There was talk of an amended social contract, in which neither employer nor employee owed allegiance to the other, and somehow the UPS negotiations had emerged as a test case of this frightening new world.

The second major issue was UPS's proposal that UPS Teamsters leave the traditional multi-employer pension fund for a newly administered, joint UPS–Teamster pension fund. The Teamsters liked the multi-employer model because it meant that their pension plans were portable if they left their jobs to go to a different company within the plan.

Kelly and other UPS managers today maintain that UPS's proposal to leave the multi-employer plan would have resulted in better pensions for Teamsters today and in the future. "I think today most people do agree that they would be better off if they'd decided to go in that direction," Kelly says. In a similar manner to how Social Security is in danger of becoming underfunded due to demographics, so, too, is the multi-employer pension plan model, which really just exists in union environments. With fewer and fewer companies being union shops today, the number of companies contributing to the multi-company plans is shrinking, leaving them potentially underfunded if the trend continues. But, again, the Teamsters positioned UPS's insistence on a company-managed pension as a power play on the part of the company, and the complexity of the issue seemed to work in the Teamsters' favor.

In the days leading up to and then during the strike, UPS continued to emphasize that part-timers received benefits at UPS, and that in the previous four years UPS had created many full-time jobs, thus greatly expanding Teamster membership. Still, the company was surprisingly tone deaf from a messaging point of view. While both of these points were true, the Teamsters' refrain *rang* true: UPS made a ton of money, and like so many other greedy corporations, it was just too cheap to pay full-time benefits. Case closed.

UPS was taken aback that its character as a good company, one that had served as an engine of economic growth and employer of hundreds of thousands of people, was being assailed around the clock on cable news networks and radio talk shows as the strike deadline neared. "You had the leaders of the Teamsters and the head of the national AFL-CIO at rallies on the national news, and we of course were horrified that anyone would talk about UPS this way," Kelly says.

THE STRIKE

Soupata, as the head of human resources during the strike, had a unique perspective. She knew Carey from when she worked as the Metro New York District human resources director and he was the head of the Teamsters New York local organization. The New York local had struck several times under Carey's leadership and she was well aware of the chaos he could create, if so inclined.

Still, she was surprised when Carey pulled the plug on negotiations when the clock struck midnight on August 4, announcing that nearly 185,000 UPS Teamsters were officially on strike. Nearly everyone expected at least one negotiating extension. As for the decision individual Teamsters faced about whether to take part in the strike, Soupata, a former member of the union herself, says, "There was always tremendous pressure on our Teamsters-represented employees. I often talked to drivers and they would say, 'You know, you're not the one in the locker room.'"

From the strike's first day, UPS was getting pummeled on the airwaves by Carey and the leaders of other unions, who lent their support despite a history of rocky relations with the Teamsters. When the workers actually walked out, UPS was unprepared not only from a messaging viewpoint but from a tactical perspective, as well. For one thing, Kelly had allowed several senior management team members to leave on vacation, assuming there would be no strike. UPS worked furiously behind the scenes to again have its last, best, and final offer put before Teamsters members for ratification, but couldn't make it happen.

As the strike went on, the advantage that the Teamsters had in the court of public opinion—here's more irony—continued to grow, thanks to the strong bonds formed between UPS drivers and customers. As Soupata puts it, "Customers were thinking, 'My nice driver is on strike, so something must be wrong with the company.'"

The public relations hits UPS continued to take were devastating. It seemed every news station or newspaper could find a sympathetic UPS client to interview. CNN interviewed Judy's Bakery in Evanston, Illinois, that couldn't send its lemon knot cookies out of state anymore. At Progressive Orthopedics in Southfield, Michigan, the strike meant a lack of materials for artificial limbs. And at St. Scholastica Elementary School in Detroit, kids couldn't get new textbooks that were supposed to arrive via UPS.

Polls continually showed, sometimes by a two-to-one margin, that the American public sympathized with Teamsters. Vice Chairman John Alden maintained in an interview at the time that Americans were sympathizing with their UPS driver, not the Teamsters' demands. "If you want to favor a corporation or the UPS driver, the UPS driver always wins," he said.

Kelly himself firmly believed that if UPS attacked the Teamsters, it was simply devouring its own—something he believed made no sense from a long-term, reputational point of view. Drivers had always been the lifeblood and the public face of UPS. He and the rest of the management team decided that it didn't want to defend the company in the news media at the expense of the rank-and-file UPS driver or loader. "If you were going to vilify the UPS driver, you were vilifying UPS," Kelly says, "and that was something we could not do. The drivers had nothing to do with that strike. If they had been allowed to vote there never would have been a strike."

Other than hoping for a rank-and-file vote, other options for short-circuiting the strike were discussed within UPS. For example, Kelly says that the management committee considered shuttering UPS altogether and coming back one, two, or three years later as a smaller organization.

Another idea floated was to make one last and final offer, and then absolutely refusing to negotiate any further. Management was also working closely with government officials about potential solutions. President Clinton's Labor Secretary Alexis Herman spoke to Kelly almost every day. One issue that was discussed was the possibility that the President, if he judged the strike to be having a seriously detrimental effect on the American economy, would invoke the Taft-Hartley Act. That would have forced the Teamsters to return to work. Eventually the Clinton administration decided not to intervene, and Herman served just a tertiary role, going over to the Hyatt Hotel in Washington, D.C., where the negotiations were held, to ensure both sides stayed at the table.

During the strike, UPS management stayed busy. A small number of highly valuable international air shipments were delivered by supervisors. Kelly was making calls and writing letters to UPS's top-100 customers. Conference calls were held twice a day with district and regional managers. To try to connect with drivers and keep the lines of communications open, a group was put in charge of creating employee communications that were sent directly to strikers' home addresses, detailing the fine points of what UPS management was offering.

The two sides finally came to a settlement on August 20, with UPS agreeing to create more full-time jobs by combining part-time positions. It was essentially the same contract UPS had put on the table prior to the strike. The agreement was played out in the media as a tremendous victory for the labor movement. As Teamsters spokeswoman Gaye Williams said on that day's *NewsHour with Jim Lehrer*, ". . . There are times when your future is threatened by corporate greed, and working people have to stand up; they have to fight back; and to do that you have to be organized."

The strike had cost the company $750 million in revenues, and many of its customers were still shell-shocked. Just two days after the tentative contract agreement was announced, Carey's 1996 election victory over James P. Hoffa, Jimmy Hoffa's son, was overturned and Carey was eventually barred from the Teamsters for life. It turned out, then, if the strike was indeed a question of character, Carey's had been revealed.

Would there be any lingering resentment toward strikers at the company where Casey always talked about being a good UPSer and a good union member? "There were some noses bent out of joint that our people would have done this, but we just had to stop feeling bad about people who, in fact, didn't cause the strike," Kelly says.

For the next few days, Kelly's time was spent regaining the trust of customers. Because there had never been a nationwide UPS strike, customers hadn't really believed it could happen, and thus hadn't prepared well. UPS held the equivalent of a management conference meeting in Atlanta, bringing the regional and district managers into headquarters for not a little soul-searching, explaining why management held firm to the strategy of not attacking the Teamsters and detailing how a deal had finally been struck.

The new competitive landscape was also discussed. For

years, many major companies had used only UPS for package delivery and they'd never been let down. Since the days of sole-sourcing with vendors were coming to an end for the most part anyway, companies large and small vowed to never again get caught with just one package delivery vendor. But the good news as the strike ended was that, at least, UPS was back in the game. Federal Express, Airborne, and the Post Office were so log-jammed that UPS was quickly back on its feet.

It was soon apparent, in fact, that Kelly's decision to take the high road during the strike was a successful strategy. Over the next two quarters, UPS bounced back and broke records for its highest revenue quarters. "The thing I'm most proud of in my entire career is the way we came back after the strike," Kelly says.

It didn't take long for the business press to take stock of UPS's comeback, or the fact that maybe the strike didn't prove such a boon for the American labor movement. George Will wrote in his syndicated column shortly after the settlement, "The strike was an attempt to rescue people who do not need to be rescued from a crisis that does not exist." In commenting on the work stoppage, Konsynski adds, "It was a sad time. I believe I saw the brand hijacked—and the drivers are the brand of the company. Would a stoppage have happened with a true voice of the entire driver community? I have little doubt who best represented the true interest of the drivers in the negotiation. And I wonder if the drivers are better served with their pension in the new arrangement."

Despite the two successive outstanding quarters, drivers were quoted in news stories as saying that it was their customers they were devoted to, not UPS. Could the "ownership company" regain the trust of its own employees?

A LEGACY OF OWNERSHIP

For those years when UPS was primarily bicoastal, with its biggest operations in Los Angeles, San Francisco, and New York, the company benefited from a brilliant system of keeping managers connected and their interests aligned in the common ownership of the company. Jim Casey had often said that the most significant factor in the company's success was that employees owned the company.

Other companies offered compensation in the form of stock to their employees, of course, but not to such an extent. "What was rare about UPS then was that it wasn't just the very top people who shared ownership of the company," Soupata says. "Offering ownership opportunities to other levels was really not done."

It was a masterstroke for operational reasons as well. By compensating managers with stock instead of cash, it helped keep cash on-hand, enabling the company to, by choice, stay out of the capital markets and maintain the unique UPS culture. It also created a very collegial workforce all pulling together in one direction. A manager starting at a young enough age—and many, many UPS managers did just that as a part-time job after high school or during college—could have a very significant cache of UPS stock at just thirty-five or forty years old.

There's a business school term called "agency cost." That's the price the owner of a company pays, and the accompanying built-in inefficiencies, for hiring someone else to manage a company. In most situations, the professional managers' interests are not completely aligned with the owner's interests, which incidentally was one root cause of some of the corporate scandals that bubbled to the surface at the beginning of this decade.

Enron CFO Andrew Fastow's interests, for example—making tens of millions of dollars investing in Enron's special purpose entities—were not aligned with the Enron board's interests.

But for decades under UPS's system, the sole owners of the company were the managers, and the managers of the company were the owners. The interests of all owners weren't perfectly aligned because shares weren't evenly distributed, but it was about as close as possible to evenly shared ownership without living in some kind of capitalistic Utopia.

Managers were encouraged to hold their shares until retirement and almost everyone did. This is partially due to the financial incentives granted by the company, one of which was an extra three percent return annually on top of market returns on shares owned. Thus, the real financial rewards came after managers left the company, a dynamic that bred a long-term view, as well as a desire to develop a new generation of leaders who would safeguard these investments.

As the decades wore on, more layers of managers were allowed into the plan. It was in 1927 that the most senior managers first started sharing equity. In the 1940s stock ownership became more institutionalized, and then the managers' incentive plan, which distributed 15 percent of operating profits as stock awards back to managers proportionate to salary, was introduced in the 1950s. New supervisors were allowed to participate in the managers' incentive plan in the 1960s. Jim Kelly, in fact, vividly remembers his first allotment: twenty-nine shares in 1967. In the 1990s, the company decided to provide drivers and other hourly employees with the opportunity to become owners, as well.

Until UPS went public in 1999, the company's board acted as the de facto market. External consultants and analysts would run financial models and benchmark against UPS competitors to act as a third-party check on the stock price the board of directors set. The board considered this input but, make no mistake, the final decision on the share price rested with the board. One of the methods UPS used was the Salomon Formula, which that investment bank's technical arm had devised as a way to help privately held companies value their companies.

The UPS board generally tried to be conservative setting the share price. It didn't necessarily bump it up a lot during boom times or downgrade the stock during the lean periods. The only time the stock ever went down pre-IPO was the quarter of the strike in 1997, when it was reduced by fifty cents, from $30.50 to $30 a share.

UPS always had the philosophy that it wanted to have consistent, smooth earnings, the theory being that a minimum of stock price volatility reflected a solid, reliable company that wouldn't let its employee-owners, or customers, down. The company's conservative fiscal policy and resulting AAA–rated balance sheet allowed managers who put all of their eggs in the UPS basket to sleep a lot better at night.

THE RUMBLINGS OF AN IDEA

UPS had always been well managed, and well-managed companies constantly evaluate how they can better benefit shareholders. At various times in the company's history there had been discussions about whether a privately held company with a limited number of owners was still the best model.

Given the climate of the times in 1999 and the number of

far-less-established firms entering the capital markets, the company's directors had little choice but to look into the idea of going public. The idea of accessing capital from outside investors wasn't unprecedented at UPS. In 1929, Casey hired an investment bank with the idea of fueling the impending expansion of UPS to the New York City environs. In a deal that gave UPS stockholders cash in exchange for stock, a new corporation was formed as a vehicle to supply much-needed capital for the expansion. Within four years, however, the full ownership of the company was back in management's hands.

In recent years, as UPS looked to make acquisitions, the company increasingly found that potential sellers were interested in stock rather than cash, to avoid immediate tax consequences. Since UPS had for years been valuing its stock fairly conservatively, it was concerned that it wasn't getting the best deal in these acquisitions.

Two key UPS advisers in the mid-1990s were James A. Runde, a Morgan Stanley vice chairman who headed the bank's global transportation group, and Harold Tanner, owner of Tanner & Co., a New York boutique investment bank. Tanner had advised five different UPS CEOs and seven different CFOs since 1976. While at Salomon Brothers in the 1980s, Tanner worked with UPS on various issues, and after leaving Salomon he was retained as a consultant to UPS for a time.

Runde, on the other hand, had called UPS CFO Robert J. Clanin in 1996 more or less out of the blue to offer analysis and advice. He was told to come on in for a meeting, *if* he didn't pester the company about a public offering. The prevailing winds eventually shifted and Runde and Tanner wound up playing important roles for UPS during the November 1999 IPO, Runde as lead banker on the UPS underwriting and Tanner as the lead adviser.

Why did those prevailing winds shift? Partly to get that publicly valued equity that could be used for acquisitions, partly to unlock the value that was contained in the company, and partly because, as Jim Kelly says, while the company was still privately held, it had been turning outward for some time.

In the fifteen years before the IPO, UPS had built one of the largest airlines in the world, gone from an almost purely domestic player to a global behemoth, and become the leading deliverer of goods ordered on the Internet. Taking the step to become a public company—with all the scrutiny it entailed— "was like putting an exclamation point on all that had gone on in the previous decade," Kelly says. "The public offering reinforced that we were outward-looking, not inward-looking, very strongly."

When Kelly and the management team decided to entertain the idea in earnest, things moved fast. On July 3, 1999, Kelly met with Runde and Richard Kaufman, also from Morgan Stanley, for three hours. Kaufman was the marketing guru responsible for drumming up buzz on the UPS offering. Further intrigued following that meeting, Kelly formed a small team to consider the idea, including a core comprised of Kelly, CFO Clanin, and then-general counsel Joe Moderow. Soupata, and, later on, Kuehn, acted as a liaison of sorts between Morgan Stanley and UPS.

A week later, Kelly and UPS vice chairman John Alden met with the bankers at an Atlanta Ritz-Carlton Hotel. On July 19,

Runde and Kaufman came to Atlanta to brief the board, after which the board debated for two days. The biggest concern during the two days of deliberation was the potential impact of the IPO on the company's ownership culture and deliberate way of making decisions, managing growth, tempering expectations, and emphasizing integrity. Managing not for the next quarter but for "the next quarter century," as Mike Eskew would later put it.

More than one person, in fact, brought up Casey's well-known writings from the 1950s, when he seemed to very much have the company's privately held structure on his mind. He wrote that the company "believed it inadvisable to broadcast all our business affairs to the world. In building this privately owned company for the benefit of us all, we have found that it pays to mind our own business and keep on sawing wood." Because of the company's long history of being privately held and the resulting sense of employee ownership at the company, another priority of Kelly's during initial talks with Morgan Stanley was formulating a communications plan to explain key aspects of the IPO to employees before word leaked out to the media or other stakeholders.

"WHAT MAKES THESE PEOPLE TICK?"

On July 22, UPS announced that it would sell 10 percent of its stock to the public, a move it said was intended to create a market for shares that could be used as the currency for future acquisitions. At the time of the announcement, with almost $25 billion in revenues, UPS trailed only Cargill and Koch Industries in revenues of privately held companies.

In a reflection of the management team's trust in Morgan Stanley and Tanner, there was not even a competitive proposal process to engage a lead underwriter or adviser. Many of the big investment banks on Wall Street that considered themselves strong candidates for the leading role if UPS ever went public, such as Goldman Sachs, Salomon Brothers, and Merrill Lynch, were surprised both by the timing of the announcement and the make-up of UPS's team of advisers. But as Tanner says, "UPS didn't care what other companies did in their IPOs or how they operated. They just wanted to do right by their shareholders and do what was best for the company."

Morgan Stanley soon enough realized that this wasn't any ordinary IPO. UPS turned out to be just as adept at gaining "flexibilities" from Morgan Stanley as it was from the Teamsters. Morgan Stanley accepted a cut for underwriting the sale well below the four percent standard. Second, UPS persuaded the bank to devise an unusual structure to meet the company's ownership traditions and preserve the power of employee-owned shares.

Shares sold to the public would be Class B stock, with one vote per share. The existing employee-owned shares would become Class A stock, with ten votes per share. In the two years after the IPO, the Class A shares gradually would become eligible to be sold, and if sold, they would become Class B shares and carry a single vote. So, even as the company prepared itself for its big unveiling to the investing public, the message was sent that the most important owners at UPS were still those persons who had invested their lives in the company for so long—the employees.

The pricing for an IPO can fluctuate wildly between the time that it is announced and the actual day of the offering. The final UPS inside valuation of the stock, owned by 125,000 current and former employees, along with foundations and company trusts, was $25.50. But given the way UPS had conservatively inched the stock up, it was clear to Morgan Stanley's valuation experts that the eventual IPO price would be significantly higher. The question was how much higher.

It had to be satisfying for the UPS management team as Morgan Stanley "kicked the tires" between July and November 1999 and grew more and more impressed. UPS had the feel of a real find for Morgan Stanley, even though it was among the most well-known brands in the world. Here was a company that was owned by thousands of experienced managers, had an almost impossible to replicate delivery network, and maintained an incredibly loyal workforce.

Some of their interactions with the UPS team gave the bankers a start, too. When Morgan Stanley looked at the company's financials, one of the first documents handed over listed the salaries of the top five UPS executives. "This is really how much you make?" one of them asked, expecting to see much higher salaries for the management team of the third-biggest privately held company in the United States. According to Soupata, "You could tell they were thinking, 'What makes these people tick?'"

In fact, UPS CEOs inevitably place near the bottom of annual rankings of CEO pay of the 100 biggest U.S. companies. At UPS, incentive compensation—the buzzword of 1990s executive pay—had little to do with the CEO and everything to do with motivating managers and employees. Casey had set that standard many years earlier.

Kuehn believes that Morgan Stanley started to recognize that it wasn't just UPS's financials and future sales that it was putting a price on, but also a set of values about how business should be conducted. While corporate values can't be seen or touched, they can be discovered indirectly, much the same way that astronomers, witnessing an intense gravitational pull on particular celestial bodies, deduce the existence of black holes. Bedrock corporate values reverberate throughout an organization, shaping behaviors and driving companies to exhibit, collectively, many of the same characteristics as people.

The incredible cultural strength of UPS would have been hard for Morgan Stanley to miss. CEOs who step down for the next person after their unspoken "term" is up. No-nepotism rules were created at the company long before most companies thought in those terms. How about during the intensive holiday busy season, when newly hired greenhorns are assisted by thousands of supervisors in an all-hands-on-deck effort to meet customer needs?

By looking deeper, Morgan Stanley also gained a much better understanding of the complexity and sustainability of UPS's global business model and its ability to branch out and create new growth opportunities. It was clear that Morgan Stanley discovered three great selling points about UPS: a great company, a compelling growth strategy, and an intriguing industry that would never go away as long as free trade existed.

UPS continually defied Morgan Stanley's understanding of

how a company and its managers behaved during the hoopla and frenzy surrounding an IPO. When the bank suggested the standard "friends and family program," in which insiders are allowed to purchase a certain amount of stock before the announcement is made to go public, UPS passed. Whatever shares executives owned as of the first management committee meeting to discuss an IPO was exactly the number they would possess on the day of the IPO. The idea was to ensure that UPS executives weren't perceived as stockpiling stock before the IPO announcement was made.

THE ROAD SHOW

The weeks of travel to deliver presentations to analysts and institutional investors—commonly referred to as "road show," but described by Jim Kelly as more like a "three-week root canal"—were grueling for UPS executives. It wasn't describing UPS's various strengths that they minded so much as the feeling that this was over-the-top, nonstop touting of the company's attributes, which went against the grain of any good UPSer raised on Casey's quiet wisdom. Which was to say just about every manager in the company. "One thing I can say about those presentations is that I landed in Stockholm three times in one day, and I'm not sure how that happened," Kelly says.

On the other hand, the road show provided for plenty of moments of comic relief when the UPS culture bumped up against that of the Morgan Stanley bankers. Because so many visits are made to so many investors, Morgan Stanley chartered a private jet for Kelly and the rest of the UPS team. "Enjoy this while you can," Kelly said to his team as they boarded the plane. "Because it's never going to happen again."

Indeed, the seeming reluctance of UPS to play the glamour game at times flummoxed the Morgan bankers. When Soupata heard where the team dinner would be held on the night before the IPO, for example, she suggested staying at the Holiday Inn because of its proximity to the New York Stock Exchange. The Morgan Stanley bankers visibly recoiled.

But other work still had to get done as the November offering approached. One of the main jobs was finishing the "red herring"—investment bank lingo for the draft prospectus, which carries a red line on the top. The Morgan Stanley and UPS teams worked together with Tanner to finish the red herring and other many compliance-related tasks.

THE BIGGEST IPO IN HISTORY

On November 10, 1999, the fuselage of a Boeing 727 Browntail was parked outside the New York Stock Exchange and a huge UPS banner draped the entrance to the most hallowed halls in American capitalism.

Almost as soon as CEO Jim Kelly rang the bell, the UPS shares, which Morgan had offered to the public at $50 a share, started shooting up in value. The market was obviously excited by a company that had ninety-two years of financial performance behind it and thousands of experienced owner-managers running it. As well they should have been, as other IPOs from that period included Pets.com and TomTom.com.

On its first day as a public company, UPS shares went up to

as high as $70.31 before settling at $68.25 at the end of the trading day. It was the most actively traded stock of the day as
investors "raced to own a piece of the company expected to deliver much—if not most—of the goods sold via the Internet,"
according to the *Denver Post*. The IPO raised $5.5 billion, a
new record. Up to that point, the biggest IPO ever was
Conoco's public offering of $2.8 billion.

The difference between what UPS valued itself at internally
and the value that investors placed on them as a public company came to about $45 billion. And again, Morgan Stanley
was surprised by the UPS culture. The bank had predicted that
after the six-month grace period expired newly enriched UPS
managers would stream out of UPS faster than vacationers out
of a Borscht Belt nightclub act. They were wrong, again.

Immediately following the IPO, much of the press coverage
following the public offering centered on the myth of the mil-
lionaire UPS driver, with the *Washington Post* topping the
hyperbole: "United Parcel Service and Wall Street combined to
create $45 billion for UPS's stockholders—among them, of
course, some of those delivery people with nice buns who run
around in those cute brown outfits." The article didn't acknowl-
edge that drivers and other hourly employees became eligible
to buy UPS shares only four years earlier. It was true that the average UPS stockholder made about $370,000 on paper when
UPS went public, but the stock wasn't evenly spread among its
125,000 holders, about 66,000 of whom were nonmanagement
UPS workers. In fewer than three years, UPS had gone from the
nadir of a nationwide strike to sitting atop an IPO that had created a market cap behemoth.

POST-1999: RETAINING THE OWNERSHIP CULTURE

With a publicly traded security to use as a bargaining chip, UPS had achieved its goal of placing itself in a much better position to make strategic acquisitions. But Kelly and his successor, Mike Eskew, would face expectations much different than any previous UPS CEO.

Instead of company employees who willingly—even enthusiastically—tied up much of their life savings in UPS, a new class of shareholders had to be considered, and they were far more interested in quarterly performance than abstract concepts like constructive dissatisfaction or dreams of turning UPS into a fulcrum of global commerce.

Since UPS became a public company, institutional investors, Wall Street analysts, regulators, and the media were free to weigh in on the company's decisions, and these voices could not be ignored. For employees, there was also the volatility of the stock price to get used to. When the market downturn of 2000 started to affect the price of UPS shares, there was great concern among all those employees accustomed to entire decades without a drop in the company's stock price.

And yet there were more owners than ever thanks to the IPO, and employee owners had seen their shares soar in value. Moreover, the next generation of UPSers will likely be motivated by the same promise of ownership as the last generation; the IPO changes nothing in that regard. Indeed, if UPS continues its successful foray into the supply chain business and other initiatives, the financial markets could reward UPS stockholders more lucratively than management ever did when the company was private, as Wall Street has no reason to price stocks conservatively.

Take Jeff Wafford, a Metro College student who is now a technical writer for UPS in Louisville. Metro College was a brainchild of Nelson, who was very interested in education reform. Students attend night classes at the University of Louisville—dubbed "UPS classes" by the students there—and then head over to Worldport to work the four-hour overnight shift. UPS staffs an overnight workforce that would be very difficult to fill in the Louisville area. Students get a good part-time job and free tuition.

BETTER THAN A BASEBALL SCHOLARSHIP

Wafford made the most important decision of his life at 2 A.M. during a long talk with a friend about what each wanted to do with their lives. Wafford, a high school baseball star from a small village in Kentucky called Vine Grove, attended Maryville College in Knoxville, Tennessee, on a baseball scholarship. Majoring in communications, Wafford didn't like the program and ended up back in the Louisville area at a community college in Elizabethtown. It was there, in the summer of 2000, that he made the late-night decision to transfer to Metro College.

Before he knew it, Wafford was working at night, going to classes he enjoyed at the University of Louisville, and receiving full health benefits and credit toward a future pension. The best part? When he received his bill from the college bursar, it said "paid in full." The second best part? Classes at Louisville heavily attended by students enrolled in Metro College end two weeks earlier than normal classes, so the students can take finals before the holiday busy season at UPS.

Before long, Wafford was managing other part-timers at UPS.

In essence, the former scholarship baseball player ended up getting the equivalent of his athletic scholarship, with one key difference. At Metro College he was earning a salary and making 401(k) contributions the whole time, and later purchasing discounted UPS stock. His only regret? "I should have been buying that darn stock from the very beginning," he says.

Wafford is just one modern day example of how UPS is still a great place for people to pull themselves up by their own bootstraps and become owners of both equity and their own futures. Tara Tichenor was a Metro College student recently promoted to a full-time management position at Worldport. Other Metro College students, like English major Eric Fraley, take their degrees and their experience and decide to work somewhere else. Either way, both UPS and the person come out ahead. "This is really the Horatio Alger company," says Tranfo, the former labor negotiator and public relations executive.

THE LINK BETWEEN OWNERSHIP AND SUCCESSFUL CHANGE

As far as corporate management teams should be concerned, the great thing about a company of Horatio Algers is that they are likely to be enormously motivated to embrace change. In a sense, the more change, the more chaos, the more opportunity—the better for them to up-end the status quo and advance through the company.

Of course, risk-taking isn't for everyone. Those UPS employees with a predilection for process and routine have no shortage of opportunities at the world's largest package delivery company.

At the same time, those with a more entrepreneurial bent can take assignments internationally or in new business segments.

In the five-year period between 1985 and 1990, UPS went through an unprecedented period of growth: it created an airline from scratch, expanded its service from three countries to more than 100, and made initial strides in automating its ground delivery methods. The term *change management* wasn't in vogue yet, but UPS already excelled in it. In fact, UPS manages change so seamlessly that the outside world often doesn't even realize when the company is in the midst of a major initiative.

"This company was purely an operations company, run by engineers," Nelson says. "Now it's a company that has become customer reactive." As UPS spokesman Norman Black says: "It's funny. There's been a set way for drivers to hold their keys for seventy years, but when it comes to big changes, this company has always been ready for it."

Changing the behavior of even one person in a corporate environment can be a challenge. Persuading hundreds or thousands of employees to adopt new behaviors, ideas, and attitudes is something else altogether. To that end, when UPS embarks on a major strategic initiative—going public or building its supply chain business, for example—it is able to successfully undertake these large scale changes without falling prey to the pitfalls (covert resistance, employee insecurity, entrenched habits and methodology, low morale) that can cripple an organization during times of radical change. One of the reasons is the long-term investment of the employees in the company.

And by far the hardest thing about managing these events is getting the hearts, minds, and behaviors of the individuals in the organization aligned with the change. To achieve this Herculean task, a leadership team must exert almost as much intellectual energy supplying a new narrative for the company as it does on making the actual change.

UPS: SUPPLYING THE NARRATIVE

When IBM issued its annual report in 2000, the text on the cover read in part:

> You're one page away from the no-holds-barred story of one year in the life of a company. It's the story of big battles, stinging defeats & gritty comebacks. Unexpected alliances, daring forays & game-changing discoveries.

Besides grabbing the attention of IBM investors, this arresting message achieved something else. It brought home to rank-and-file employees that, following a huge drop-off in corporate orders after Y2K and the bursting of the Internet bubble, the company was in the fight of its life. During 2001 and 2002, IBM righted itself, outperforming competitors with new products like self-managing servers and microdrives.

UPS also excels at supplying its employees with a narrative that motivates them to exhibit the behaviors that are best for the company. From its three-minute driver PCM meetings every morning to its three-week orientation period, UPS gives its employees an excellent grasp of the company's "big story." The story's emphasis, of course, remains on the business principles and integrity of founder Jim Casey.

And the ownership company seems to have a lifelong hold

on its employees. Like many retired UPS executives, Lea
Soupata will spend some time in Florida, do some work with
the Annie E. Casey foundation, and perhaps do some teaching.
When asked to name any retired UPS executive who has chosen to launch another career—say, starting a niche business in
the transportation or supply chain arenas—she couldn't name
one. "Everybody is coming up to me and saying, 'What are you
going to do now?'" Soupata says. "If I wanted to work full-time
I'd still be at UPS; I loved it."

So, in the end, what is the ownership company? One might
say it's a place where a hard worker of integrity can build an
impressive nest egg. Another answer would be a highly disparate group of people of different backgrounds, educations,
and aspirations drawn to a culture of success. A third response
would be that it's a place where many people just love to come
to work.

UPS RULES FOR THE ROAD

The Ownership Company

- **Emphasize training.** UPS training sessions and corporate schools that expand employees' "toolkits" are held all over the world for seasoned UPS executives and new employees alike. The company is so committed in this area that it spends more than $400 million annually on employee training and development.

- **Lead employees out of the comfort zone.** Jim Casey famously believed that employees *want* to leave their respective comfort zones, and that the best way to successfully promote in-house is to give managers just enough responsibility so that they are almost, but not quite, over their heads.

- **Believe in your employees**. If a company is invested in its employees, then those workers will return that investment fivefold. In today's business world where employees are typically treated as free agents, a company that seeks to promote its own employees and creatively supports its employees' hopes for the future (UPS's Metro College in Louisville, for example) is going to earn a lot of devotion from its workforce.

- **Promote from within.** Every CEO at UPS has risen through the ranks, and it's the job of managers to groom their successors. The result is a team of managers with an intimate understanding of each other and the business, which breeds a level of trust because the person above you has likely performed your job well enough to be promoted.

9

Synchronizing Global Commerce, One Supply Chain at a Time

"Synchronized commerce is the aspirational view of the perfect supply chain. It's the supply chain done right."

—MIKE ESKEW,

UPS CEO

ONE-STOP SHIPPING IN HEBRON

At 1100 Worldwide Boulevard in the town of Hebron, Kentucky, just across the Ohio River from the once-bustling port that put Cincinnati on the map two centuries ago, stands a glistening white, fortress-like distribution center of the future. A large sign at the entrance trumpets in large, white block lettering: HONEYWELL. "This ain't UPS," insists Paul, proprietor of a local cab company, as he tries to find UPS Supply Chain Solutions for a customer. "UPS is down the road."

Like baseball umpires and senior prom chaperones, supply chain consultants best serve their purpose going unnoticed. This particular mirage is obviously effective, but eventually dissolves in light of the tiny "UPS Supply Chain Solutions" sticker on the glass front door.

Here in the Hebron distribution center, custom-built in 1997 for Honeywell, UPS conducts a symphony in automation and global distribution management five days a week, three shifts a day: 710,000 square feet of futuristic scanners, pneumatically powered sorting lanes, battery-powered forklifts, and RFID-ready pallets that speed Honeywell's consumer products group shipments around the globe.

The center's size is such that several of the more fitness-conscious workers eschew a gym membership in favor of a calorie-burning constitutional around its mile-and-one-half circumference during lunchtime. But the fact that this is the biggest and most high-tech UPS Supply Chain Solutions facility isn't the most impressive thing about it, but rather how it smoothes out the bumps in Honeywell's supply chain world.

In a late 2005 speech, UPS CEO Mike Eskew described his vision of the supply chain this way: "Commerce used to be three distinct movements, three separate flows. The first was the flow of information—the order-entry process. The second movement was the flow of the goods. And the third was the money. Those movements are no longer distinguishable."

Those three components of Honeywell's consumer product group's supply chain—goods, information, and funds—operate in much closer harmony since UPS took over distribution of marquee brands such as Prestone® antifreeze/coolant, FRAM® oil and air filters, and Autolite® spark plugs. Delivery cycle time per order has shrunk dramatically; order accuracy is 99.5 percent; Honeywell has saved millions in transportation costs; and the group's distribution-per-unit cost has fallen each year.

In the mid-1990s the consumer products group, part of Honeywell's transportation systems group, served its 10,000 North American retail and service customers out of five 1950s distribution centers dispersed throughout the U.S., Canada, and Mexico.

Honeywell decided it needed help coordinating shipments headed to the same area of the country, differentiating outgoing orders en masse and balancing inventory among the five cramped, low-ceilinged warehousing locations. UPS proposed a radical solution in 1995: Shutter all five distribution centers and build two modern, UPS–run distribution centers—one in Fernley, Nevada, to serve the western U.S. and a bigger one in Hebron to serve other worldwide clients. UPS's proposition: Cut down supply chain complexity and improve service levels.

UPS faced significant challenges, as Honeywell itself had many demands from their customers. For instance, one customer uses automated electronic data interchange (EDI) transmissions to "see" product on its way, and wants suppliers to get on board with the technology. Another customer wants to meet with UPS and Honeywell every week to review inventory and forecast.

The reason that these companies place so much pressure on Honeywell is that the car maintenance market is a mature one. Simply put, annual growth for the consumer product group must come from lowering prices for customers, who can pass the savings on to their customers.

GOING MY WAY?

The biggest variable in lowering the group's costs is more efficiently transporting its products from Hebron and Fernley to customers through its network of hundreds of carriers.

Unlike the UPS small package business, the supply chain group doesn't own a whole lot of trucking assets. UPS uses a custom transportation management software program to ensure that the consumer product group's shipments don't go out in piecemeal, half-full loads, which drives up shipping costs.

How does UPS do this? Trucking is ruled by two major delivery methods: truckload and less-than-truckload (LTL). The standard truckload, which can hold fifty-two pallets (about 100 cases of goods make up a pallet), costs one set price. LTL deliveries are charged by the pound. It's sort of like ordering a full meal versus à la carte. Now do the math. There comes a point when an LTL shipment becomes more expensive than simply paying for an entire truckload. That demarcation point is typically about fifteen pallets.

Say, for instance, that a large retailer places ten orders each week for delivery to 100 different stores around the country. The trick is to get those ten orders on as few truck routes as possible, meaning faster delivery and lower costs.

If one of the orders is a thirty-eight-pallet order of transmission filters to its stores in the Pacific Northwest, for example, UPS will pay for an entire truckload, but still have space for fourteen pallets of some other product. Now, say a small retailer in Oregon needs ten pallets of a different product. UPS will try to get those ten pallets on board the first truckload. If

UPS can do that, it will be using forty-eight out of the fifty-two pallets—not too bad, but not great.

If UPS can find another four pallets of product going to that same part of the country, a client can really start saving money. The more shipments that make it onto an already-paid-for truck-load, the more per-unit-cost distribution plummets. UPS also uses what's called pool shipments. For example, if our four pallets of product are not going to the exact same part of the state as the forty-eight pallets, UPS will pool the shipments together for as long as possible on a full truckload, get as close to the end-customer as they can, and then break the order up and send the four pallets on a separate carrier by LTL.

Through its transportation software, UPS uses complex algorithms to figure out which of the carriers are offering the best rates, which routes they are using, and which additional consumer product group shipments match the departure time and destination of an outgoing truckload.

Things get infinitely more complicated because one important factor is the cost of holding up a truckload to wait for additional LTL shipments—because it costs money to hold a shipment, both in driver time and potential late fees. Truckers can under current federal regulations drive no more than eleven hours in a row. So if a trucker is waiting around to fill out a load, that's less driving time left over.

Managing LTL deliveries will get much easier for UPS in the future due to its 2005 purchase of freight carrier Overnite, a $1 billion-plus acquisition that qualifies as UPS's biggest purchase ever. UPS now has its own LTL solution (UPS Freight) for companies like Honeywell and thousands of other companies that aren't so big.

The ability of UPS to manage the transportation element of its customers' supply chain stems directly from the "stretching" of its core package delivery product and a century of transportation know-how. For UPS, integrating the transportation aspects with inventory has been a focus, and product moving through a massive distribution center like Hebron is a journey in and of itself.

WHAT GOES OUT MUST COME IN

In supply chain-speak, UPS first manages the incoming inventory from manufacturing plants. In other words, what eventually goes out must, at some point, come in. Although many companies keep their largest manufacturing plants in the U.S., they also produce products in—where else?—Asia.

At one end of the Hebron distribution center one encounters a "test lab," a sort of lab for testing products made overseas that aren't quite ready for prime time yet. Like a just-learned golf swing, the rub inherent in outsourcing manufacturing to China or India is repeatability. Early on in any outsourcing relationship, companies are never quite sure of the quality level of what's going to come in, meaning that the consumer product group—through UPS—needs to check and recheck incoming shipments. At the test lab, a team of UPS technicians use high-powered microscopes to examine various products manufactured elsewhere.

If UPS drivers are the face of UPS, then industrial engineers are its central nervous system. UPS engineers are masters at envisioning the intersection of industrial engineering and mechanics, and in Hebron they push themselves and their teams to do things better and faster for clients.

Engineers' fingerprints are all over the facility, from the first "picking area" to the newly constructed catwalks that allow workers to reach the third-story sorting belts and monitor package movement. For example, UPS managers thought that the distribution center of the future shouldn't be rife with the oppressive smell of standard propane gas-powered warehouse vehicles. Subsequently, the trailers and forklifts in Hebron all run on eight-hour batteries, and about 300 giant batteries are mounted on a side wall, continuously charging.

A few years ago, UPS managers started a competition of sorts at the distribution center to launch projects to save clients money. It's viewed by employees as part job responsibility and part sport: Think of a solution to an engineering problem that a client doesn't even know it has.

For instance, one solution was the simple wooden pallet. Clients often supply the pallet, and rarely consider what happens to them once they get to a distribution center, especially since the wooden slats often get damaged by heavy items at the bottom. So at Hebron, UPS hired a carpenter who spends his days listening to hard rock music and rebuilding slats on pallets. That's hundreds of pallets that UPS can now use again to send products out, and save clients money—sometimes thousands of dollars.

THE SEARCH FOR GROWTH OUTSIDE OF THE SMALL PACKAGE BUSINESS

The 1997 strike, a painful blow to the company's reputation and bottom line, also served to highlight the fact that after ninety years of business, UPS was still almost totally dependent on its domestic small package delivery business, earning almost ninety-five percent of its revenue from that source. UPS had been very aggressive in building out its global network once it made the decision to expand internationally, but that investment hadn't yet started returning significant dividends.

Its inability to find other sources of domestic growth in the years preceding the strike wasn't for lack of trying. In the early 1980s, when UPS found itself with a surplus of cash on hand, it formed a diversification team to drum up ideas for growth outside of its core small package delivery service. Based on the company's core competencies in industrial engineering, management, and operations, the group identified several businesses in which UPS would seem to have a competitive advantage. One of these was operating hotels. UPS went ahead and bought a majority share of the Copley Place Hotel in Boston and a Hyatt in Dearborn, Michigan, among several other properties. It also considered purchasing security firms like Pinkerton and Brink's, the concept being that managing vehicles and drivers on time schedules on a set network of stops was squarely in UPS's sweet spot.

But the hotels were sold off shortly after they were purchased, and the other ideas were quietly dropped. UPS had determined its cash was better used in launching a nationwide overnight air service in 1983 and a rapid expansion of its international small package business a few years later. Meanwhile, after Oz Nelson became chairman in 1990, UPS continued to roll out new package delivery services, more than thirty between 1990 and 1992. These products were more or less successful, yet brought the company ever closer to tapping out revenue streams directly related to small package delivery. Coupled with the fact that those years in the early 1990s were also marked by enormous losses in the company's international operations, UPS was hungrier than ever for new revenue streams. After fighting so hard to serve the entire country with its small package business and then building a global network, the company wasn't about to stop looking for growth opportunities.

At about the same time, a few logistics-type services UPS offered started to take hold as offshoots of UPS's core small package business. One of these was truck leasing. Another was a service called Martrac, in which refrigerated UPS feeder trucks would carry California fruit and vegetables to the East Coast after delivering small packages to the West Coast. This served to reduce expenses as well as balance equipment.

In late 1993, UPS formalized a potpourri of these different one-off services into a line of business called World Wide Logistics, which focused on helping customers with warehousing, inventory management, fleet management, customs brokerage, and distribution.

Though it hadn't quite articulated its strategy this way yet, UPS was taking the first step in changing its mission from meeting the small package needs of customers to enabling global commerce. Building its supply chain business would turn out to be perhaps the most dramatic new strategic direction for the company since shifting from retail service to common carrier service in 1952.

Visitors to Louisville today who tour UPS's three-million-square-foot supply chain complex might be taken aback at what the logistics business looked like just ten or fifteen years ago. For example, before UPS technology customers had their laptops and LCD players stored in world-class, high-tech distribution centers, they were placed in plain old, vanilla warehouses. Before warehouses, there were storerooms. Before storerooms, there were, according to UPS's David Abney, "essentially closets." And before closets, there were . . . car trunks?

That was the case for years at Sonic Air, which was the first significant acquisition for the logistics arm of UPS. While World Wide Logistics was essentially an organic creation within UPS (though it contained several small acquired businesses), Sonic Air was aggressively courted and then purchased in late 1994 to provide UPS with a capability that the other big package delivery companies already offered: same-day delivery service. UPS Sonic Air Service launched on April 12, 1995, and it was no surprise that FedEx started FedEx Same Day in response on June 1 of that year.

EXTRACTING THE HIDDEN VALUE WITHIN SONIC AIR

Sonic Air was the brainchild of Ray Thurston, and it maintained two separate businesses. One was the high-profile, same-day delivery of packages on commercial airlines that had attracted UPS in the first place. If an organ needed to be flown from Phoenix to Chicago for a critical transplant, for example, Sonic Air would book the next commercial flight available, and then deliver and pick up the organ from the airport.

From blood samples to a high-powered executive's pair of golf shoes, Sonic Air would deliver anything, including a pair of sneakers to Michael Jordan when His Airness once found himself without a pair on game day. But, ironically, it was Sonic Air's second, and far less sexy business—hauling computer parts around in car trunks—that led to UPS's service parts logistics business, and made the wider company believe that it could succeed at logistics in general.

The UPS strategy group understood that Sonic Air's same day service could easily be expanded to transport computer parts, since field technicians for HP, IBM, and other companies were invariably stuck waiting for parts to arrive so they could fix employee and network hardware. Like the other companies in that business, field technicians for these electronics companies carried "trunk stock," literally as many computer parts as they could store in the trunks of their cars. Then it was off to a certain section of, say, metro Atlanta, to install the parts. Though the field technicians consistently met their same day goals, they couldn't carry much inventory and often found themselves out of a certain crucial part, whereas technicians on the other side of town might have plenty of that part, but no time to deliver it crosstown. Overall service, needless to say, wasn't that efficient.

According to Abney, who became head of Sonic Air after it was acquired, Sonic Air's innovation was to purchase storage space all over metropolitan areas to store computer parts, called "field support banks," so that in each important customer area, couriers could quickly restock. "Once our strategy team was really there doing our due diligence, we saw this very small, very new innovative solution, and that ended up driving the service parts logistics success we would continue to have after that," Abney says.

UPS expanded Sonic Air's "smart couriers" service, which made basic repairs on printers and other computer hardware. Though Sonic Air was kept separate from World Wide Logistics at the time to avoid smothering the small, newly acquired company, it soon became apparent that the business of same day delivery of computer parts to technicians was an excellent fit with the inventory management capabilities of the World Wide Logistics group.

Big technology companies based in Silicon Valley were under more and more pressure to get replacement computer parts from their warehouses in California to the East Coast. Since even then Louisville was an all-points air hub for UPS, the idea was that if UPS held some of its customers' inventory of computer parts, the needed items could be sent out that much more quickly to corporate and residential customers, via the adjacent air hub.

UPS believed that if it could provide "end-of-runway" warehousing at its Louisville air hub, and then send parts out to local field support banks, big tech companies would jump at the chance to outsource their computer parts logistics business to UPS.

And that's exactly what happened. "What the end-of-runway location allowed us to do is make a pickup out of the warehouse as late as 1:00 A.M. and have it anywhere in the U.S. by early A.M., 10:30 A.M., noon, or end of day, depending on the customer's needs," Abney says.

In 1999, the UPS strategy team saw right away that the high-speed, high-intensity, high-value computer parts and repair business could be improved upon once again. One of the factors that often made the IT repair business a weeks-long ordeal was the seemingly straightforward, but in practice complicated, dynamic of connecting the technicians with the parts. By the time companies received deliveries, it was sometimes past 10:00 A.M. At the customer location, often the equipment would get there well before, or well after, the field technician, and the repairs would have to wait because the technician would leave the site to move on to another customer. But if a technician could pick up replacement parts at a UPS facility, repair work could start at 7:30 A.M. or 8:00 A.M. So, UPS developed field stocking locations, like the one in Lyndhurst, New Jersey, where technicians could come and get the parts they needed as early as 7:00 A.M.

Another "big idea" soon followed. Like many large companies, UPS employed hundreds of technicians to service its own employees' computers. Soon enough, the idea of leveraging these technicians to create a full-fledged repair center for customers' computers led to a burgeoning business. So for some companies, like Toshiba, UPS started doing the repairs right in Louisville, sending the fixed machines out as quickly as possible from Worldport.

THE NEW MISSION: ENABLING GLOBAL COMMERCE

The expansion of the SPL business also coincided with the broader post-strike imperative to find new growth opportunities. In the months following the strike, Jim Kelly had led a strategic planning meeting to investigate various models for the future of UPS. Market share had been lost, and gloomy projections for the next decade of package delivery abounded. Much discussed, according to Jack Duffy, then vice president of the UPS corporate strategy group, was modeling UPS after the IBM model. IBM had realigned its business with a services unit but still retained some of its legacy (hardware) business. "It was a watershed discussion," says Duffy. "There were people who thought we had stretched the package business as far as we could go. After all, it had been, what, ninety years at the time."

And yet those ninety years had provided an incredibly successful product to build on. It's not surprising that the strategy group decided that UPS should stretch its "core capabilities," tied to its delivery infrastructure, network planning, operational excellence, industrial engineering firepower, and growing IT integration.

By 1999, UPS had revised its charter to change the company's mission for the first time in its history, from serving customers' small package needs to enabling global commerce. It was, in fact, a completely natural evolution for UPS for several different reasons.

First, UPS's relationships were so deep with some longtime customers that it understood the entirety of their supply chains and had valuable suggestions to make. Second, the logistics business could piggyback off of the hard-won national infrastructure UPS had already built. Third, UPS's expanded global footprint and success in becoming a technology company gave it the geographic coverage and technological firepower to delve into the complicated world of logistics, where services have to be perfectly timed and configured to meet a company's individual needs.

Against this backdrop and given the new corporate mission, the UPS strategy group knew it couldn't stop with the service parts business, so it also pushed the development of other services within World Wide Logistics, such as the group's transportation capabilities. As Bob Stoffel, head of UPS's Supply Chain Solutions unit, puts it, "Anyone can run a warehouse, but not everyone can manage a complex supply chain network, and that's where we had an advantage over a lot of other people trying to do logistics." The company, for example, noticed that lots of the full trucks coming into warehouses UPS managed left empty. They also witnessed endless waiting around by drivers. UPS convinced some customers to let it run their dedicated fleet, with the goal of more efficient fleet management.

STRATEGIC ACQUISITIONS HELD
TO RIGOROUS CRITERIA

With the decision made to aggressively enter the supply chain outsourcing market, UPS starting acquiring logistics companies in order to build the business up in a reasonable amount of time. It eventually spent more than $2 billion acquiring nearly thirty companies. Among them: Challenge Air Cargo in 2000; freight forwarder Fritz in 2001; Mail Boxes Etc. in 2001 (rebranded as The UPS Store in the United States, Canada, and India); First International Bancorp in 2001; Menlo Worldwide Forwarding in 2004; and LTL carrier Overnite in 2005. Integrating these companies into the greater UPS has been done cautiously, "because we would just have crushed them under our weight," Eskew says.

Overnite, branded as UPS Freight in May 2006, provides the company a major piece of the full-service puzzle. The LTL business has historically been very fragmented, with no clear leader. And the market is huge: plenty of companies need to send more than a few small packages, but less than a truckload. As with Honeywell, UPS's traditional involvement with the LTL sector was buying third-party capacity for customer orders that didn't fit into its small package business. Now much of that business can be claimed by UPS itself. As of late 2006, UPS was busy applying its company standards to the business and supplying UPS Freight drivers with DIADs.

The Overnite acquisition was atypical for UPS in its size and scope but typical in terms of how strategic it was. Despite the fact that about 75 percent of all mergers and acquisitions fail to create lasting value, UPS has settled into an acquisition strategy that research shows increases the chances of a successful merger. The defining aspect of this strategy is maintaining a rigorous set of merger criteria that the company tests every potential acquisition against. Prospective acquisitions must compete in an attractive market, complement UPS's skills, and drive internal growth.

A study published in March 2003 by the *Harvard Business Review* shows that one winning acquisition strategy is to engage in a consistent pattern of multiple acquisitions in a short time period. The study examined 7,475 acquisitions made by 724 U.S. companies between 1986 and 2001. The researchers found that the 110 "frequent buyers," or those firms that bought more than twenty companies during a fifteen-year period, outperformed infrequent buyers (those that bought one to four companies) by a 1.7:1 ratio, and decisively beat pure nonbuyers by a 2:1 ratio. The "serial acquirers" evaluated mergers in a similar manner to UPS, as well: a disciplined set of rigorous acquisition criteria, consistent processes, and a focus on both financial and cultural metrics.

With the mergers, the supply chain arm of UPS was up and running at full steam, and the company's vision of transforming itself to move beyond small package delivery to enabling global commerce was becoming a reality.

UPS TODAY: CONFIGURABLE SOLUTIONS TO ENABLE GLOBAL COMMERCE

Today, as its supply chain business has become more integrated into the company, UPS thinks of the way it serves its customers as "one-to-one." This phrase has several meanings, one of which is that UPS offers one integrated network to facilitate the global transportation and distribution of goods for its customers, and those customers need not make any differentiation between UPS's small package business, UPS Supply Chain Solutions, UPS Freight, etc. Technically, sometimes those divisions do exist, but UPS is working hard to make those lines fade and simply offer a full suite of products to customers.

The competition will be fierce, of course. While thousands of niche players can successfully take over one or two components of these twisting and turning supply chains, the clear emergence of just four or five global players is the most likely scenario in the next few years. There are just not that many companies with the worldwide reach to manage every aspect of a global supply chain. As Kurt Kuehn says, "We're generating customer value and fair returns with a highly integrated network that no one else can really match, because no one else has one hundred years to spare."

Exactly who those competitors will be remains to be seen. Whereas UPS views supply chain services as a vital set of options to deliver configurable solutions to clients, FedEx has for the most part stayed out of the supply chain outsourcing tussle, believing that the company is best served by building up its individual transportation units, like FedEx Ground. UPS and FedEx, in fact, see the future of global commerce quite differently, and the reasons are at least partly historical.

FedEx, founded on the strength of one man's idea, remains unconvinced of a business model where numerous partners—and sometime competitors—must work in concert over the long haul. UPS's Jim Casey–inspired, consensus-driven approach, on the other hand, thrives on that very sense of cooperation and communications across multiple vendors and intersecting supply chains. DHL, for its part, has chosen the opposite end of the spectrum and has thrown itself into virtually every area of contract logistics. UPS, one could say, has struck a middle ground with its offering of configurable solutions related to its core transportation business.

UPS also sees the potential profitability from supply chain solutions differently than both FedEx and DHL. One key to profitability in supply chain services is to parlay the solution developed for a customer such as Honeywell and standardize it across a broad customer base. "Supply chain work is more customized and more fragmented than small package deliveries, but we're getting better at coming up with solutions that you can apply to different clients," says Raj Penkar, head of the supply chain group's solutions practice.

A second key is using the "deep dive" into customer supply chains to increase small package revenue. In Hebron, not far from the distribution center that UPS runs for Honeywell, for example, UPS houses designer shirts, digital cameras, and $1,000 linens that a Web retailer sells. UPS obtained the supply chain assignment from the company first and retained the Web retailer's small package business after that—exactly the kind of relationships that Eskew has in mind for the UPS supply chain and small package businesses.

This will likely increase as purchasing and procurement managers continue to internalize the supply chain concept. At a conference of corporate procurement managers that he attended in October 2006, for example, Kuehn noticed that wringing value out of the supply chain was a hot topic of conversation, whereas a few years ago the supply chain was really more a topic for academics. He's seen the same dynamic at UPS's biannual Longitudes conferences. "When we first started Longitudes, the academics really dominated the conversation when it came to subjects like the supply chain, and now the practitioners have more to say," Kuehn says.

SUPPLY CHAIN OUTSOURCING: NICE WORK IF YOU CAN REPLICATE IT

Various estimates place the potential global supply chain market at upward of $3.2 trillion, compared to a global package delivery market of less than one-tenth of that. Of course, that $3.2 trillion number is a little like saying that Kellogg's market for Froot Loops is all six billion people on earth, or that the potential market for *Time* magazine is anyone on the planet who can read. Logistical limits cap the amount of cereal that can be profitably manufactured, magazines printed, distribution centers staffed, or customers marketed to.

UPS views the logistics marketplace more like a $350 billion pie. Given that UPS's current slice of that pie is about $8 billion, there's plenty of room for this part of the company to expand. In fact, the supply chain unit is growing at about a 10 percent annual clip, while UPS's small package growth is averaging about 6 to 7 percent growth per year.

What is fueling the growing market for logistics outsourcing? Macroeconomic forces are creating complex supply chains that snake through all kinds of new markets—and companies need help managing them.

Among the trends redrawing the routes of global commerce: the outsourcing of manufacturing to Asia; a more integrated global trading community; an IT revolution that enables anyone to order goods from anywhere; explosive growth of consumer classes in China and India; and new discoveries of raw materials in South America and Eastern Europe. The volume of global trade in goods and services rose at an average annual rate of 6.6 percent over the past decade (1997–2006), according to the International Monetary Fund. This growth rate is even more robust when "goods" is considered as a stand-alone category: 10.9 percent growth for 2004 and an estimated 7 percent and 7.6 percent in 2005 and 2006, respectively.

There are many good examples of these trends when one looks at UPS's roster of international customers. One is UPS's work with National Semiconductor. Back in 2000, National Semiconductor hired UPS to manage its global supply chain, after several years spent working with a competitor. With manufacturing facilities in the United States, the United Kingdom, Malaysia, and China, National Semiconductor wanted a high-tech global distribution center easily accessed from its manufacturing sites, a place with an educated but affordable workforce.

The company today consolidates its five billion analog

semiconductor chips shipped each year at UPS-run global distribution centers in Singapore and China. In fact, about 90 percent of National Semiconductor's entire inventory goes through these facilities. From the initial order to delivery, UPS's 135 employees can get National Semiconductor's items anywhere in the world within seventy-two hours.

The automation at the facility rivals that found at the Hebron, Kentucky, facility. The PKMS warehouse management system, developed by Atlanta-based Manhattan Associates, ensures that as soon as National Semiconductor receives an order from a customer on its servers, it comes into the UPS system as well. The inventory status of each box going through the warehouse is visible to both National Semiconductor and UPS, so the exact time that the goods will leave the distribution center is known.

And the PKMS system breaks each order into categories—full order or partial order—so that the employees can easily decide how to treat each order. With a full order, for example, not a box has to be opened; the entire set of boxes is sent straight to the loading area. Partial orders mean that boxes are opened and sent to another area to be combined. To top it off, twenty-four-hour customer service is located in the facility, and National Semiconductor's clients also can track their shipments on UPS.com using a special code.

"The moment we scan the box, it's entered into the UPS system and their client knows what's coming," says Mike Tan, the senior operations manager at the distribution center. "And in the event that there is a long chain of clients and the last one in the chain is the consignee, that's okay too; that information will be in the system."

Another example is Hitachi. Hortense Vasquez is a logistics executive for Hitachi Global Storage Technologies (Hitachi GST). In 2003, Hitachi Ltd. purchased IBM's storage technology division and continued the relationship IBM and UPS had established in 1995. The newly merged company worked with UPS to consolidate the Hitachi and IBM facilities. This new distribution network was reduced from seventy facilities to just fifty-four, eliminating unnecessary duplication. Hitachi GST's customers continued to have real-time visibility of their shipments and Hitachi GST was able to keep less inventory.

UPS also adds value throughout the Hitachi GST supply chain. In a solution akin to the repairs UPS performs under its service parts logistics (SPL) offering for a computer company in Louisville, UPS has the capability to reconfigure hard drives according to Hitachi's specifications before they are sent to the customer. UPS calls it "light manufacturing." The process is extremely helpful in Hitachi's ability to meet demand and it eliminates the need to do this work at the manufacturing facilities.

Europe, in fact, is a big part of UPS's supply chain strategy. One of the strategic goals for UPS over the next few years is to take advantage of a sort of "reverse outsourcing," coming back from China. According to UPS's Frank Sportolari, some companies in Germany and the United States have brought manufacturing back closer to their end-markets, finding that the labor savings in going to China were subsequently erased by transportation, fuel, and supply chain costs. UPS hopes to use its European network for more cross-border ground volume if some of these outsourcing operations end up in Eastern European countries like Poland, Romania, and Bulgaria. According to

Sportolari: "Some of these Eastern European countries aren't yet ideally positioned for business, but they'll be there very soon."

MORE THAN THE SUM OF ITS PARTS

The idea behind UPS's service parts logistics business is—as quickly as possible—to connect IT technicians with the computer parts needed for a repair of a consumer's or businessperson's hardware. For some customers, such as Toshiba, UPS takes the customer service call and technicians fix end-users' computers right at a UPS facility, meaning that Toshiba doesn't actually get involved in day-to-day repairs.

One of UPS's biggest service parts logistics clients is IBM. The computer giant does not warehouse a single spare computer part designated for repairs; it's all managed by UPS Supply Chain Solutions. The Lyndhurst, New Jersey field stocking location is one of the biggest of the 120 such locations that serve IBM. The UPS field stocking locations are only as big as they need to be, and some locations have only one employee.

In addition to IBM, six other critical parts companies are serviced from Lyndhurst. Through these customers, Lyndhurst provides computer parts to hospitals, police stations, the New York City Department of Education, the financial services and insurance industries, and even the New York Stock Exchange.

Dave De Leon, a distribution operations manager who handles Lyndhurst and several other field stocking locations, is a former IBM logistics expert recruited by UPS to handle the IBM account. De Leon's engineering challenge is to maintain top operational speed. Most parts ordered go out to IBM's customers on the same day, many within the hour. The most urgent service parts requests contractually require UPS to have the part out the door in twenty minutes or less. After consulting with UPS industrial engineers about time-saving procedures, a chute was installed so IBM technicians picking up parts and the UPS shipping clerk handing them out wouldn't spend three, five, or ten seconds in conversation during handoffs.

The Lyndhurst field stocking location operates twenty-four hours per day, seven days each week. After all, when it comes to repair, you just never know. IBM customers like the New York Stock Exchange, for example, can't afford to be down for even a minute, so it keeps a room of technicians armed with UPS-transported IBM parts at the ready.

The process is simple enough. An executive at, say, a major bank can't start her desktop PC. Her company help desk diagnoses the problem, but needs a new motherboard, monitor, or maybe even hard drive to fix the machine. The help desk contacts the IBM call center (actually UPS) for the part, generating an automatic printout about fifty yards from De Leon's desk. An employee takes the printout straight to the loading area, where the order is quickly pulled, packed, and sent on its way. The Lyndhurst facility, because of its size, carries just about every IBM part, so IBM customers all over the Northeast receive replacement parts from here.

Not only is the Lyndhurst team fast, they are also creative. When New York City's transit workers went on strike during the holiday season in 2005, impacting the Manhattan stocking locations, the Lyndhurst field stocking location became the focal point for all IBM service parts going into Manhattan. The parts were flown into Newark Airport from IBM's manufacturing plants, consolidated and sorted in Lyndhurst, and then driven by courier to the New York Waterways Ferry. Couriers were also stationed at the ferry landing in downtown Manhattan and, upon arrival, the parts were walked off the ferry and handed over to them.

Because the vehicles on the ferry never actually had to enter the city, UPS didn't have to comply with the four-passenger rule that was in effect in Manhattan between 5:00 A.M. and 11:00 A.M. Three UPS Supply Chain Solutions managers in Manhattan oversaw the process, and there were no service failures during the strike.

After 9/11, a field stocking location on Cedar Street, right across the street from the World Trade Center's South Tower, couldn't provide customers with parts. Working with FEMA's control center in the Meadowlands, the Lyndhurst team developed a plan to deliver emergency parts for IBM into the city. By September 13, the team was delivering parts into Manhattan for IBM.

ALL ROADS LEAD TO LOUISVILLE

In Louisville, the service parts logistics shop is going strong. There are twenty-one hours of coverage in UPS's technical repair area. One major building is completely turned over to the Toshiba account. According to Rocky Romanella, a longtime UPSer and senior manager at UPS Supply Chain Solutions during its formative years, what UPS does for Toshiba is the best example of Eskew's vision of UPS positively affecting its customers' customers. Toshiba laptop owners calling in a technical problem reach a UPS call center and are directed to drop off their computer at the nearest UPS Store. The UPS Store ships the machine Next Day Air to a UPS facility in Louisville, and by 5:00 A.M. the laptop is in line to be repaired. If the customer is lucky, the problem can be fixed and sent back that very day for next day arrival. UPS technicians, typically with two-year degrees when hired and then certified to repair whatever machines they work on, repair four Toshiba laptops at a time in the Clean Room, the innards of the computers spread out before them, ready for reassembly.

But it's not just Toshiba laptops being fixed in Louisville. Digital media projectors made by In-Focus are repaired here, too. A bar code scanning company has seen the average time for repairs shrink by several days. One customer even sends in dot matrix printers for repairs, and several UPS technicians had to read up with antiquated manuals to do the job.

When UPS was a retail delivery service transporting furniture from Macy's and Gimbels to customers sixty years ago, the retailers' goods sat next to its competitors on the ride through city streets. Today, UPS has re-created that dynamic, with competitors' laptops, projectors, and digital cameras side by side in a UPS distribution center.

PREMANUFACTURING: A NEXT GENERATION HIGH-TECH SERVICE

The horizon for the high-tech supply chain market has become much broader than service parts logistics. For example, UPS sells another major service to clients, which could end up dwarfing service parts logistics: premanufacturing. Because UPS has such an extensive delivery network, the supply chain group tends to add its value later in the supply chain, during the distribution phase (think Honeywell), or even after the sale, during the repair phase (think Lyndhurst and Louisville). But not always.

Computer manufacturers are also hiring UPS to improve vendor managed inventory through a service called Supplier Management. This helps customers manage international suppliers with more accountability and better control, earlier in the supply chain, regardless of time and distance.

One customer wanted to own its inventory as late in the manufacturing cycle as possible to cut down on warehousing and other costs. While it's at the UPS hub, the customer doesn't pay a dime for it. Once it enters the manufacturer's building, ownership is passed to the customer.

UPS, not surprisingly, puts these hubs right next to the manufacturer if at all possible, allowing them to order up parts for new units on extremely short notice, anticipating that they will reach the manufacturer in just a matter of hours. This process means that the customer has virtually no warehousing or early-on distribution costs for all the products it treats this way.

One of the catchwords of the supply chain industry is "visibility," the ability of a company to see what's happening in its supply chain and where the inefficiencies are. With UPS performing supplier management, the customer knows exactly how many parts have been pulled and units assembled at any one time, and of course it knows how long it takes to manufacture its own computers. With all of this visibility, the customer can basically order up computer parts from UPS as it needs them, on a day-to-day basis if it wants to.

In addition to its high-tech focus, there is another area that deserves special mention because of its potential for growth and importance in the world: health care. The UPS Supply Chain Solutions health care business is a very different one than its high-tech business.

THE HEALTH CARE SUPPLY CHAIN: A DIFFERENT KIND OF BUSINESS

In a UPS distribution center complex there sits an enormous vault. The 1,600 pallets stacked inside the fourteen-inch concrete reinforced walls don't include precious metals, priceless works of art, rare artifacts, or Berkshire Hathaway stock certificates.

Instead, the vault holds items far more important to its intended recipients: highly controlled pharmaceuticals for those suffering intense pain from injury or disease.

The drugs are owned by Pennsylvania-based Endo Pharmaceuticals, but stored and distributed by UPS Supply Chain Solutions. Endo, a specialty pharmaceutical company that concentrates on pain management, outsources just about all fixed asset-based functions and owns no "bricks and mortar" assets.

Endo owns its pain products, the associated patents, and the IT systems that allow Endo to plug into its "big brothers" like UPS and SAP. Endo owns no manufacturing equipment or plants, office buildings, warehouses, or trucks. It has more than 1,000 employees on the payroll, but two-thirds make up the sales staff that in 2005 rang upward of $800 million in sales. As Daniel Carbery, Endo senior vice president of operations puts it: "We're basically a big pharma without the big balance sheet." In other words, take all the quickly degrading plants, machines, and vehicles that many big pharmaceutical companies wished they didn't possess, walk away from them, and what's left is Endo.

Endo's business model of concentrating solely on its core business processes of developing and marketing pain-relieving drugs and related therapies relies heavily on UPS correctly storing and distributing products that include such household names as the Lidoderm® patch, Percocet® tablets, Percodan® tablets, and Frova®, as well as recently approved products Opana ER® and Opana®. In fact, according to Carbery, some of his peers in the pharmaceutical industry shake their heads in wonder (and skepticism) at how deeply Endo and UPS are tied into one another.

The two advantages UPS gives Carbery are scale and its laser focus on performance metrics, which is critical when the FDA and other regulatory agencies come around. "In the last few years, we've watched UPS become a health care company in the way that it handles our and other companies' products, and it's pretty incredible," Carbery says. "We like to think that they've learned some things from us about handling sensitive pharmaceutical products and we've really benefited from them."

The speed at which Endo can now get its products to market following FDA approval has proven a boon for Endo's sales and its relationships with big retailers like Wal-Mart and Rite Aid. Because the profit margins on newly released, much-clamored-for generic versions of prescription drugs are so high, the big retailers want those products on their shelves the very same day that FDA approval comes in, if possible. In response, UPS and Endo have virtually eliminated the period between FDA approval of a generic drug and distribution to Endo's sales network. Even before approval, a cache of Endo's product will be stored, ready to be distributed.

AN INTERRUPTED VACATION

In 2005, Endo's generic version of oxycodone, a controlled drug that is very cumbersome to ship because of the special distribution requirements and sheer number of regulatory forms that have to be managed, was the subject of an extended legal battle, and therefore couldn't be sold to the public.

Then one day, a fax came over the transom notifying Carbery that the case had been decided in Endo's favor. Carbery contacted Endo's distribution manager, Lisa Walker, who was just about to go for a swimming pool dip on a well-deserved vacation. Walker immediately contacted UPS's Jackie Kiefer, the site manager for the Memphis Supply Chain Solutions facility, and the product launch machinery went into motion. A few hours later, Kiefer and her team had organized the shipping documents, notified customers of an impending delivery, and set up the transportation from Memphis to three major customer sites. By midnight, the shipments were out the door; twelve hours earlier, no one at Endo or UPS had a clue that the legal decision was even going to come down that day. Most major shipments of newly approved product take about twenty-four to thirty-six hours to arrange.

In another instance, Endo finally acquired a product in 2004 that it had coveted for some time. The company that had owned the product kept it in a Memphis distribution center across town. When word came that the deal went through, UPS was able to retrieve the entire product cache and ship it the same day from its own Memphis facility. "The irony of this is that we don't even own a distribution center, but with UPS we've become a world-class distribution company," Carbery says.

As a trusted partner, UPS might also question the business case for a new initiative Carbery wants. A good example is a new electronic ordering system that will allow Endo's products to advance through the health care supply chain—from manufacturer to Memphis to wholesaler to retailer—much more quickly. Initially, UPS thought the new system might cause more problems than the old, paper-based one. But now that the system is about to roll out, UPS is pushing Endo to move more quickly. "You know," says Carbery, "when I look at UPS's history, when it decides to do something, it focuses on it and it crushes it. That's what I think it will do in health care."

A DIFFERENT MINDSET

As it does for high-tech companies, UPS can help its health care customers reconfigure their supply chains to more efficiently distribute health care products. The only catch was that in order to acquire this ability UPS had to unlearn, starting in 2000, some of the very axioms that took nearly a century to master.

Today, the health care supply chain practice is the fastest growing within the supply chain group, and had about 100 clients as of January 2006. The group got its start in Canada, where Livingston made its name in the 1990s as a health care logistics outsourcer. Bill Hook, who in late 2006 was vice president of global health care logistics for UPS, was a key manager at Livingston when UPS acquired the company in 2000.

Cracking the U.S. health care supply chain, however, presented a much greater challenge than doing business in Canada. Prior to 2000, UPS had very little knowledge of the financial and cultural nuances of health care outsourcing. Says Endo's Carbery, who had a front-row seat when UPS purchased Livingston, "UPS bought Livingston to get into the health care and pharmaceutical space, but that first year it looked to me like UPS was thinking to itself, 'Um, what exactly did we just do?'" By the end of 2003, UPS's health care market share was lagging behind that of its other supply chain businesses, because, according to Hook, "We were treating the ultimate client the same way as any other receiver of a package. UPS had to become more of an integrated partner with the customer."

UPS had devoted nearly a century of operational excellence to treating all packages essentially the same, so it's not surprising that this idea that the health care supply chain was unique took a little getting used to.

For one thing, the ultimate end-user was a medical patient. Delivering narcotics or plasma isn't the same as carrying sneakers or garden hoes or art supplies. As Mark Hale, a UPS director of health care operations in Louisville, says, "Sending the wrong pair of running shoes is one thing; packing the wrong box of pharmaceuticals could be a disaster for the people taking the medicine."

The patient factor also necessitated a home delivery "personal touch" element that was somewhat foreign to UPS. For example, more than 3,000 customers of Canada-based Baxter Corporation suffer from chronic kidney failure, and receive their prescribed dialysis therapy medicines and fluids at home from UPS-managed couriers.

The couriers deliver up to thirty thirty-two-pound boxes of fluids into patients' homes every week, and often spend an hour or so unloading the boxes and helping to set up and test the equipment so the customer can self-administer treatment.

The couriers understand, according to Baxter supply chain director Brent Hodgson, that they are playing an important role in helping these patients avoid weekly trips to a clinic or hospital, thus improving their quality of life. Needless to say, spending that amount of time working with one residential customer is not your standard supply chain solution. As Hook puts it: "In health care, sometimes you have to make a choice that's not the most efficient financial decision, but that is still the right decision."

Despite these challenges and the initial difficulty gaining health care market share, UPS management became convinced of the enormous market potential for health care supply chain services if the company just played its cards right.

Romanella, too, started to believe that, in the same way that the company's historic reputation for industrial engineering and integrity convinced high-tech companies to trust UPS as an honest broker for repair logistics, the company could parlay this goodwill to make inroads into health care. And, perhaps, UPS could even contribute solutions to America's health care crisis.

Motivated both by the market opportunity and the potential to help fix the country's health care system, UPS completed a 550,000-square-foot health care distribution center in Louisville in 2005, followed by an approximately 700,000-square-foot joint health care/high-tech center that was completed in late 2006. In a sense, UPS is now on the front lines of making health care more affordable in this country.

INCREASING RESPONSE TIME

Less than a mile away from the six buildings of the high-tech UPS Supply Chain Solutions campus stands its health care supply chain building at 1920 Outer Loop Drive. Nearly 100 percent of the building has now been filled with goods from seven different customers.

The Louisville health care facility has more compliance hurdles to constantly pass than any other UPS facility. For example, it must periodically provide the FDA with data proving that it is keeping medical products at the right temperature. The climate-controlled side of the building is constantly tested for temperature and humidity, as UPS can take no chances that any drug or sensitive device will be exposed to extreme heat or cold. In 2006, a new refrigerated section of the health care facility opened for "cold chain" products, as they are referred to in supply chain lingo. Cold chain items, such as certain pharmaceuticals and vaccines, need to be stored in temperatures between two and eight degrees Celsius.

In several football-field-long rows in the climate-controlled part of the distribution center are stored such things as antimicrobial dressings, compression bandages, and antifungal moisturizers, among others. While most supply chain facilities rely on the employees to double-check themselves, in any of the company's health care facilities there are several levels of human checks for each item that is picked and boxed.

One of the greatest reasons for growth at the Louisville facility is that orders can come in as late as 11 P.M. to the health care distribution center, get packed, and get shipped from WorldPort up to 2 A.M. or 3 A.M. Emergency orders can be taken to Worldport and put on a departing flight for morning delivery. Doctors, nurses, and patients can then track the en route package via the Web, and alter the patient's medical treatment based on knowing when the items are going to arrive. As Hale says, "We've designed the health care product distribution to skip some of the typical UPS steps."

ENABLING GLOBAL COMMERCE MEANS ONE-TO-ONE SERVICE FOR CUSTOMERS

In the end, providing configurable solutions is the most natural of evolutions for UPS. After all, nearly a century ago, Jim Casey placing messenger boxes in Seattle taverns to save patrons a walk to the Western Union station certainly subtracted a step out of sending a message, and was a way of moving "information" more efficiently.

Today, UPS doesn't spend time expediting Western Union messages, but instead Honeywell oil filters, IBM chips, and Endo pain medication.

Here's a thought: Maybe it's the business world that is finally inventing terms for what UPS has been perfecting for a century. And perhaps another century from now, the business world will play catch-up again and coin more phrases for what UPS is doing today: serving customers one-to-one.

UPS RULES FOR THE ROAD

**Synchronizing Global Commerce,
One Supply Chain at a Time**

- **Import fresh ideas when they are needed.** In the 1980s, the company hired hundreds of IT professionals when it was transforming itself into a technology company. Today, as the company ventures into supply chain solutions, new expertise is required to manage the complexities of these business processes.

- **Adaptation.** UPS has survived a century of competitors and other external threats, because it has evolved with business. A willingness to explore new business models and embrace transformation has saved the company more than once.

- **All aboard.** To move a company forward, the future vision must be communicated to employees. One or two meetings introducing a new product or line of business won't do the trick. A sustained, coordinated series of messages and events must provide evidence that this vision is the key to a company's health—and to employees' self-interest.

10

One Company, One-to-One

"Our horizon is as distant as our mind's eye wishes it to be."

—JIM CASEY,
UPS Founder, 1954

ON THE GROUND IN THE WORLD'S BIGGEST MARKET

Daryl Tay, an up-and-coming UPS marketing manager from Shanghai fluent in Mandarin, Cantonese, and English, once dreamed of attending business school in the United States. But that was before Tay started working for UPS, before UPS became wholly owned in China, and before China turned into the most exciting spot on earth to conduct business.

Now Tay is part of something big, participating in a phenomenon that MBA students at Wharton or Harvard only get to read about in case studies. Between 2004 and 2006, UPS's presence in China grew from 500 to 4,000 employees. The company experienced 50 percent growth in its export volume from 2004 to 2005, the year it bought out its joint venture with the Chinese

[259]

government-owned Sinotrans for $100 million. Measured on a purchasing power parity basis, China in late 2006 qualified as the second-largest economy in the world after the U.S.

In fact, one could say that at the start of UPS's second century of business, Tay and his colleagues work in the company's ultimate proving ground. After all, where better to measure the company's ability to enable global commerce than what will likely become the biggest consumer market in the world?

Building an airline, developing a comprehensive global presence, transforming itself into a technology company, ramping up its logistics business—all of these watershed achievements over the past two decades have put UPS in excellent position in 2007 to meet the many challenges of succeeding in China. The question is whether the company can harness and organize all of its services to treat the Chinese customer as if it's UPS's only one—the heart of CEO Eskew's one-to-one vision. "Our aspiration, in a sense, is to grow the service idea that Jim Casey had when he started the company," Eskew says, "to the point that the needs of our customers are so well understood that providing the right kinds of services is almost instinctive."

ONE-TO-ONE IN CHINA

Understanding Chinese customers—big and small companies alike—enough to serve them as Eskew envisions will take all of UPS's collective experience and the local know-how of young UPS managers like Tay. "You know, people think of China as one market," Tay says one rainy day in late May 2006, traveling north on a highway between Shenzhen and Guangzhou, one of the busiest trucking corridors in the world. "But down here in southern China, the customer is cooperative: 'Oh sure, stop by, we'd love to talk about what UPS can do for us.' But up north in Shanghai, it's very different. It's a more demanding, more advanced environment: 'I'm the customer, give me what I want.' "

Tay's van passes Korean Kias, Chinese Geelys, and Japanese Hyundais; German-made Audis and Passats pass the van. There are no gaps in the buildings here, no tourist shops, barely even a tree or rice paddy. Along the 100 miles of highway between Shenzhen and Guangzhou, many of the sprawling factories look big enough to be airports. The Guangdong province is home to more than 2,000 manufacturing plants, and every day thousands of economic skirmishes are waged between global behemoths like Apple and Dell, Panasonic and Hitachi, Nike and Reebok, Sears and J.C. Penney, Dollar Tree and Wal-Mart, Li & Fung and Luen Thai. As a result, we can all have our flat-screen televisions, iPods, blue jeans, Happy Meal toys, and basketball sneakers more cheaply than ever before.

At noon tens of thousands of workers, clad in their standard-issue blue uniforms, trudge along the main road dotted with construction projects. The worker housing in Guangdong, typically adjacent to the plants and factories, is of the cinder-block dormitory style. Bused in from the country's interior rural villages and leaving children behind with grandparents, the former farmers and fishermen soon find themselves working in some of the most technologically advanced factories and distribution centers on earth.

At the UPS Supply Chain Solutions consolidation warehouse in Yantian, for example, just a few kilometers from the port and the South China Sea, UPS uses warehouse management software, package tracking, and EDI technology to help customers combine hundreds of disparate orders from suppliers all over Asia. Each spring, in preparation for the Christmas holiday season Sears purchases goods from scores of vendors that manufacture goods in, say, 100 different factories all over southern China.

Instead of Sears managing these piecemeal shipments itself, UPS receives all the different orders and organizes them into consolidated shipments. UPS will transport the goods from the vendors' manufacturing plants to the Supply Chain Solutions warehouse and, later, to a waiting cargo freighter. Sears doesn't even own many of the goods until UPS validates that an order has been correctly filled. For big companies like Sears, the one-to-one promise is that UPS will one day provide visibility of a company's in-transit assets across all modes—goods coming in from suppliers, orders coming in from customers, funds moving across borders. Another service in the future would be the ability to redirect extra inventory in that Yantian warehouse to a company thousands of miles away whose customers *do* want that inventory. "With total visibility, companies will have the ability to bring 'dead' inventory back to life," says Kuehn.

Some inventory can die a very slow, painful death, particularly those products with a long, complicated supply chain. To save that inventory, UPS can't customize for every customer, but can configure a solution with services like supplier management and Trade Direct. "Take Christmas tree lights being manufactured in China," says CIO Barnes. "You have freighters, decentralized warehouses, suppliers, thousands of stores. Within a complicated supply chain like that, there is ample room to drive costs down by skipping steps and doing something like shipping ornaments, stands, and lights all together directly to stores."

And it's not just a question of creating big-picture, macro improvements for customers. UPS also uses its century of industrial engineering know-how to make small tweaks. For example, every layer of packing material costs Sears more money. UPS pickers and loaders can pack more goods on a pallet than Sears' vendors could ever do, and they use less bubble wrap and other materials to do so. It's a small difference—but it's the small things that make customers feel as if they are experiencing a unique, one-to-one service from UPS. That's what Jim Casey realized 100 years ago, and it's what UPS still understands today.

A BRIDGE TO GLOBALIZATION

Eskew's one-to-one vision also means enabling companies based in China to connect to the rest of the world, as well as serving those running their supply chains through it. Most of the world's goods still ship by ocean freight, and companies that do elect to ship from one of two Shenzhen area ports, Yantian and Zhujing Kou, sometimes face days of delays. Customs management technology isn't particularly up to date and the manifest paperwork often isn't automated.

The challenges in UPS building and meeting customer demand in interior Chinese cities like Chongqing, a Yangtze River port that now boasts the world's biggest population, are quite different than in the coastal areas. There are no seaports inland and nearly 100 airports in the interior of the country without paved runways, so reaching potential customers there is incredibly difficult. "The real question in China over the next ten years is the infrastructure going west; how that is going to be built," says Sebastian Chan, a managing director at UPS Supply Chain Solutions in Shanghai.

UPS, not surprisingly, plans on being a big part of the spread of goods to China's interior. Much in the same way that UPS spent much of the twentieth century fighting regulatory battles in the U.S. to procure the rights to serve all contiguous forty-eight states, the company is primed for a similar challenge in China.

In late 2005, in fact, UPS launched domestic express delivery service within China, and as of early 2006 served 330 cities across China. No matter how isolated some areas of the country, a population of 1.3 billion and a rapidly growing consumer class means that companies with products to produce and transport, both domestically and for export, will follow. Eskew, who served as president of the U.S.-China Business Council from 2004 to 2006, puts it this way: "When I worked in West Germany for UPS in the 1970s, the people on the other side of that wall didn't know how people in West Germany lived. Today in China because of the Internet and popular culture, everyone knows how the upper middle class lives."

To really create the kind of one-to-one customer intimacy in China that it enjoys in the U.S., though, UPS needs to concentrate on four factors: increase its presence, improve its service quality and internal processes, keep improving training for all UPS employees in China, and expand its sales force.

For example, to increase its presence, UPS will begin in 2007 the construction of a second major Asian air hub at Shanghai's Pudong Airport, to join the flagship Asian air hub at Clark Air Force Base in the Philippines. A Shanghai hub is important for UPS because there are so many goods flowing out of China to the U.S. and Europe that the volume UPS handles really just depends on how many planes it can get off the ground. Air capability is also important within Asia, where unlike in the relatively cozy confines of Europe, one can't exactly truck products from southern Asia to northern Asia.

As with UPS's business around the world, the company's ultimate footprint in China will be driven largely by market forces, by the degree to which commerce keeps growing in China and customers find UPS services advantageous. Much like Abney's premise that UPS needs more viable customers in Africa before it can invest significantly more resources there, UPS's presence in China will match customer demand. "When we are at our best for customers, they grow with us because they truly have a market advantage," Barnes says. "That dynamic goes for American customers, Chinese customers, customers anywhere around the world."

ONE-TO-ONE WITH CUSTOMERS IN CHINA

Hong Kong is UPS's most mature market in China, meaning that it's a useful barometer with which to project how UPS could be serving customers on the Chinese mainland in the years ahead. As Kurt Kuehn points out, many companies in China today can't even afford the computer and Internet access to use UPS's technology tools.

In Hong Kong, though, where UPS has been doing business since 1988, customers are highly sophisticated in their business practices and demand excellent service. Part of meeting customers' high expectations is anticipating their needs, what Eskew calls, "Being ahead of the customer." The best practices gleaned and emerging trends spotted from serving its huge customer base helps UPS stay ahead of customer demands. Eskew and the rest of the management team also talk to hundreds of customers every year, and frequently hear two refrains: they want focused attention on their business issues, and a one-stop solution. "When it comes to the process of developing solutions and products, I think we get to the customer, in aggregate, quicker than anyone else," Eskew says.

YesAsia.com is a good example. It has considered UPS a business partner since Day One. In 1998, Priscilla Chu founded the company with her husband as a way to get Chinese DVDs and books to San Francisco for Chinese and Chinese-Americans who, like themselves, did not live close enough to San Francisco's Chinatown to easily obtain them. The first month they had just 100 orders, but then business picked up when Chu sold 3,000 CDs of a recording by the popular Chinese singer Faye Wong.

Business kept growing, because no other Web site offered such a comprehensive and eclectic mix of Asian pop culture items, and the couple moved the business to Hong Kong in 2001. Each day, YesAsia.com now sends between 1,500 and 2,000 orders with UPS. It also uses UPS to ship from its source offices in Japan and Korea to the hub in Hong Kong.

From there, YesAsia.com distributes all over the world via UPS, with 40 percent of the company's sales coming from the United States. Chu says that YesAsia.com is growing so fast that the UPS services they need keep changing. Chu and her husband now use a UPS product called WorldEase to route, consolidate, and distribute the inventory within the United States. In another twist, YesAsia.com ships express to the States but ships by UPS ground service within the U.S. "UPS's competitors can't do what it is doing for us, at a reasonable cost," Chu says.

In the future to stay successful, YesAsia.com will need services that continue to, as UPS executives put it, "shrink the distance" between YesAsia.com and its customers. That might mean using Delivery Intercept, a new UPS service which allows the in-transit "un-sending" of a package that the sender mistakenly sent to the wrong person or, say, inadvertently placed a confidential document in. When a customer chooses this service through UPS.com, the information stops the package and when it's scanned at the destination the UPS employee is told to reroute the package. In fact, on-the-fly changes in information about an individual package will one day be the norm. An architect working at home who receives blueprints every other Tuesday, for example, will be able to enter into UPS.com instructions re-routing his standard delivery to a hotel in New Orleans where he is attending a conference. A huge part of one-to-one is UPS allowing customers to treat *their* customers like they are its only customer.

Another recently introduced service that increases the likelihood of a successful transaction is Proactive Notification, where UPS would phone a YesAsia.com customer and notify them that it is delivering a package the next day. "Our future services, enabled by technology, are all about shortening the distance between the buyer and the seller," says John Nallin, the UPS IT executive.

Like YesAsia.com, thousands of small-to-medium-sized entrepreneurs toil away in Hong Kong trying to shorten the distance between them and their customers, but entrepreneurship is also thriving on the mainland. One of the fascinating aspects of UPS operations in China is both their immaturity and enormous potential. For an American equivalent, think of UPS just starting to hit its stride as a common carrier in the 1950s.

"Our operating managers have always had an enormous level of responsibility in the United States," says David Abney. "But in China, it's tough to pick up the phone and call a colleague and say, 'Hey, how did you handle this?' Because the truth is there is no one who has done it before."

All throughout Asia, in fact, questions often arise about issues that have been settled matters for years in the U.S. and Europe. In a UPS Asia Pacific regional meeting in May 2006, for example, region head Ken Torok and Tom Murphy, who in late 2006 was head of UPS Asia Pacific's air operations, were talking about the relative merits of switching a weekly flight from Malaysia to another Asian country with more of an "Open Skies" policy. This kind of flexibility and openness to change will be important if UPS is going to be able to structure itself to meet customer demands not just in China, but throughout Asia.

In Japan, for instance, UPS must act according to sometimes opaque business cues. According to Torok, a contract with a Japanese company can be signed and, for some reason, the organization may continue using its "former" vendor for months, making the transition to UPS seemingly package by package. For UPS and other companies, it's also famously difficult to market new products and services in Japan, for Japanese and non-Japanese sales forces alike. Not only is it very difficult for a sales professional to schedule a meeting with a decision maker in Japan, but the cultural premium on self-effacement precludes an aggressive pitch to a senior executive. As Brian Cusson, senior vice president for UPS's North Asia district, phrases it:

"Doing business in Japan is just a little more complicated than anywhere else."

It's a delicate balance, one that Janice Chan, UPS's director of business development for the North Asia district, has figured out how to maintain. Chan has initiated a North Asia district-wide sales program called "Give Me Five," in which UPS sales representatives throughout the North Asia district obtain leads for their colleagues on the Japan sales team. When packages are delivered to a Japanese company operating in, say, Korea, the salesperson in Korea will take down the information of the Japan-based company that sent the package and turn the information over to the Japan sales team. The goal for each North Asia sales team member is to provide five especially promising leads. This is a way for other Asian UPS operations to pitch in and help UPS grow in Japan without committing any business or social faux pas that would hamper UPS in the country.

The aspirational view of the one-to-one philosophy is personified in young UPS employees like Chan and Tay, professionals who understand that UPS must sometimes tread lightly in local business environments. In fact, a crucial aspect of UPS's one-to-one strategy turns a phrase that has gained currency in recent years on its head. UPS believes that as a company it should "Think Local and Act Global." In other words, even as UPS strives to be considered "of" the countries in which it operates and stay relevant from a local service standpoint—a Chinese company in Shanghai, a Belgian company in Brussels, a Turkish company in Istanbul—its ultimate goal is to help companies in these countries connect to a market that is nothing less than global. To this end, as it has forged its global brand,

UPS has drastically reduced the number of expatriates in its international operations, to the point where they make up less than one-tenth of one percent of the international workforce.

FULFILLING THE ONE-TO-ONE VISION

Growing up in Indiana, Eskew wasn't thinking so much about one-to-one as he was one-*on*-one. Like any good Hoosier, Eskew played a lot of hoops as a kid. "When it comes to being a Hoosier, basketball is a pride thing," he says. Besides playing basketball and golf, Eskew also worked in his father's surveying company, where he first began to notice how things worked, why some methods of doing something took longer than others, and that he had a knack for problem-solving.

To Eskew, after all, that's all the one-to-one vision means: providing a solution to a customer's problem, whether that means sending a small package next door, moving freight in less-than-truckload (LTL) mode, or filling an entire cargo ship. As envisioned by Eskew, UPS's strategy of one-to-one means that UPS will help customers solidify new markets, differentiate new product lines, improve customer service, enhance productivity, and strengthen their cash positions.

The factors that led to the company's one-to-one vision are rooted partly in Eskew's past as a UPS engineer, in which he spent much of his time configuring optimal routes for UPS feeder trucks, package cars, and airplanes. As a young UPS engineer, Eskew was fascinated that by tweaking the systems in, say, Washington State, packages in parts of Oregon or Idaho could be delivered more quickly.

This past success in shaping the network to produce better customer service helped form Eskew's belief that the one-to-one vision is a realistic and achievable one. When Eskew first joined UPS in 1972, its business was much simpler; in fact, the built-in repeatability of the service—one regulated rate chart no matter how big or small the customer, ironclad schedules for pickup and delivery, weight limits that were strictly adhered to—was the genius behind it. There were only two numbers worth studying for the typical UPS manager: stops-per-on-road-hour and pieces-per-hour. If those numbers were high enough, all would be right in the UPS universe.

That, as the saying goes, was then.

Today, UPS is providing an array of supply chain solutions for complex, global corporations. As the division of labor around the world becomes more dispersed, companies can optimize portions of their supply chains by moving order centers to India, manufacturing to Vietnam, and distribution to Singapore, just as a few examples. But someone needs to put it all together. Years ago, UPS would have had little appetite—and no capability—to synchronize all of these elements of commerce for a company. But that's exactly the capability that the one-to-one strategy offers.

WHAT ONE-TO-ONE MEANS FOR FUTURE INTERNATIONAL GROWTH AT UPS

The one-to-one strategy hasn't been fully understood or embraced by various UPS stakeholders, Wall Street analysts among them. The response by these critics has been that the one-to-one philosophy sounds as if it attempts to provide all things to all people, potentially requiring costly customized services or heavy investment in assets. But UPS is convinced that its strategy of combining its transportation services with a defined, configured set of supply chain solutions is the "sweet spot" for the company moving forward.

As it manages one of the world's most well-known brands, operates the world's eighth largest airline, and is one of the country's largest users of railroad cargo space, three factors allow UPS to successfully maintain its balance at the nexus of global trade: the ability to stay ahead of the prevailing wisdom about which markets will grow, the discipline to be prudent about investing precious resources, and the responsibility to be a positive social force in those areas it does invest in.

UPS's recent investment in Poland, for example, illustrates that it can be a successful catalyst and make prescient strategic moves ahead of the prevailing wisdom. In 2005, UPS Europe spotted an opportunity. One of the leading parcel and express delivery companies in Poland, the Warsaw-based Stolica, was looking to expand its ability to deliver express packages via international air. Conversely, UPS, which had recently become wholly owned in Poland, was looking for a way to get up to speed quickly and broaden its growing Polish customer base.

UPS's strategy team came up with three good reasons for acquiring Stolica: it would strengthen UPS's operations in Poland and Germany that would feed one another; Poland had a much larger economy than the other ten Eastern and Central European countries that had just been allowed into the EU, meaning plenty of profitable packages coming down the pike; and UPS Poland needed a much stronger footprint in Poland. In May

2005, the trigger was pulled and UPS is now neck-and-neck with DHL for market leadership in Poland.

At the same time, UPS has to be prudent. After all, it doesn't make the rules and it can't control which countries thrive. Something that always puzzles Abney is how otherwise savvy business managers and business students think that UPS, being a socially conscious company with a very powerful brand, should leverage those strengths to create more infrastructure in underdeveloped parts of the world, the logic being that business will follow.

Abney sometimes guest lectures at Emory University's executive MBA program in Atlanta, which has a strong international bent and draws students from all over the world. Though UPS has entered into a joint venture in Nigeria, he still gets the same question over and over again: "When is UPS going to do the same thing in Africa that it's done in other parts of the world, like Germany and China?"

Abney, sitting in his fourth-floor office at UPS headquarters, sighs. "You know, we are not a leading indicator," he says. "Our network has to reflect the global economy. If we get too far ahead of the market in any one country, our business will become unsustainable."

THE FUTURE EVOLUTION OF THE UPS BRAND

The now-iconic "What Can Brown Do for You?" advertising campaign was a very successful method of communicating a new UPS message to the public, and in a sense, was a way to articulate the one-to-one vision for a mass audience. To its

credit, UPS realized in the late 1990s, before many other companies, the newfound power of the customer. Whereas he or
she used to represent the passive end of the supply chain, the
consumer, through tools like the Internet, became the origina-
tor of the typical transaction, and therefore what goods were
produced and how they were delivered.

In 2001, UPS sought a way to incorporate this idea into its
brand. Larry Bloomenkranz, vice president of brand management and advertising, was one of the executives in charge of
managing the evolution of the brand. All manner of options were
discussed, and when the company officially changed its brand
identity in 2003—just the fourth time it had done so in its
history—it marked a new beginning. "The old logo, with its
small package, was great for a company that ran 'The Tightest
Ship in the Shipping Business,'" Bloomenkranz says. "But for a
company enabling cross-border commerce, helping customers
achieve their strategic goals, that company needed a new brand
platform." The new shield—minus the package—represented
the expansion of UPS capabilities.

Like most companies, UPS today thinks about how it will
continue to grow in the future and how that growth will affect
its brand. But unlike most companies, UPS's broad capabilities
and global reach means that it is able to consider a wide array
of business opportunities. It's quite amazing, in fact, to consider
the many varied paths that UPS has in the past considered following.

Says Eskew: "At one point we thought, 'Well, we're pretty
good at managing data centers, we have two that are the best in
the world, should we manage people's data centers?' We eventually decided that probably wasn't a good idea." During the

dot.com boom, UPS even thought about throwing itself into the online grocery business before UPS engineers concluded that the business model didn't offer enough scale. In fact, diluting the brand is a very real danger for a company that introduces as many new products and services as UPS does today. Expect the brand to stay very close to the end-customer.

ONE-TO-ONE IN RETAIL

Even as UPS dominated the package delivery market for so many years, its history of largely delivering packages for businesses meant that—aside from the ubiquitous UPS driver—the company was very difficult for consumers to conveniently find and use. It became clear that for the typical consumer to see the one-to-one value proposition, UPS needed accessible retail access points.

In the United States, UPS relies on approximately 40,000 drop box locations, over 8,800 third-party pack-and-ship locations, and more than 1,000 customer centers attached to UPS facilities to service the needs of retail customers.

In 2001, UPS acquired franchisor Mail Boxes Etc., Inc. (MBE) and, on April 7, 2003, more than 3,000 Mail Boxes Etc. locations in the United States chose to re-brand as The UPS Store. The stores remain locally owned and operated by franchisees, and provide shipping services and a portfolio of business services to their customers.

In 2004, the year after the branding change, MBE opened more than 500 new locations of The UPS Store in the United States—a record for the company, and particularly impressive for a nearly quarter-century-old franchise. The UPS Store, while used primarily by small businesses and individual consumers, offers another avenue for creative ways for UPS to serve its customers. For some of UPS's service parts logistics (SPL) customers, for example, computer technicians can receive parts as early as 7:00 A.M. at selected The UPS Store locations, well before the first deliveries from UPS would arrive at a typical place of business or home. This gives technicians a crucial head start in fixing customers' machines. The UPS Store also gives the company a presence at "special-venue" sites, such as college campuses, hotels and convention centers, and military bases.

Outside of the U.S., UPS now has more than 4,800 retail access points, including more than 1,300 locations of Mail Boxes Etc. and The UPS Store. The UPS Store brand had its international debut in both Canada and India in 2005. UPS has introduced other retail sub-brands such as UPS Express in China, the strategy being to make UPS as convenient as it is reliable in all parts of the world.

HOW IT AND IE WILL CONTINUE TO INFORM ONE-TO-ONE

Going forward, serving customers one-to-one means using IT to create a more flexible operating model and a wider range of services. That's why the company's historic interplay between IT and industrial engineering will continue to be critical.

In Baltimore, at UPS's Operations Research Division, an intriguing, long-running experimental marriage between IT and IE is playing out that continues to pay dividends.

Jack Levis has led Operations Research since 1996. He and Dr. Ranganath Nuggehalli, together with their crew of mostly youthful math theoreticians, spend their days devising and testing complex algorithms to figure out new ways for UPS to cheat time. Adding routes within China, extending next day air service to suburban Moscow, or providing more reliable overnight deliveries from Los Angeles to downtown Atlanta—somebody has to figure out how all of these services can be offered efficiently enough to be profitable.

The quest to shave a few more seconds from a driver's shift seems quaint, almost retro at the modern UPS, replete with package flow technology, redundant mainframe computers, and DIADs with GPS capability. But there are still all kinds of opportunities to save time. For example, the Operations Research team continually works on ways to optimize driver routes and minimize the number of left-hand turns a driver makes, because left-hand turns mean wasted time at intersections.

In fact, it's almost impossible for UPS drivers right now to take the most optimal route when delivering their packages. Why? The potential number of different routes, or "tours," a driver can take is based on how many stops are needed. Three stops? No problem; there are just six possible delivery paths. But four deliveries mean twenty-four different delivery paths. As the number of stops increases, a phenomenon that operations researchers call a "combinatorial explosion" kicks in: With twenty-five stops, for instance, there are more than thirteen trillion trillion potential delivery paths. If one assumes that with the help of a very fast computer a researcher could evaluate four billion paths each second, it would still take 122 million *years* to compute every different delivery path combination.

In other words, it's essentially impossible to break down the different delivery possibilities through standard information technology, because computers don't possess that kind of brute computational power. "We're having trouble even fashioning a method to make all of these calculations, because the potential data is most of the transportation information in the world," Dr. Nuggehalli says.

But the Operations Research mathematicians can devise algorithms, a kind of repeatable computational shortcut that builds on itself, to solve certain parts of these brain-teasers, allowing the company to design more efficient driver routes.

In a speech on August 1, 2005, to attendees of the Asia Technology Summit in Hong Kong, Eskew talked about technology's role in creating customer intimacy and how it can create a much deeper, richer connection between UPS and customers. He described how when he joined the company in 1972, the company wanted to improve, yes, but it wanted to improve UPS's processes, and just keep perfecting those sacrosanct ways of doing things. By improving UPS, customers would benefit from lower rates. But technology and process improvements were not about improving the customer's experience. Today, according to Eskew, those days are "long gone." UPS has one goal: serve its customers how they want to be served.

There are many ways to use this technology. UPS.com is the most direct link with most customers, and millions every day track their packages on the Web site. But there are also shipping tools that speed customs clearance; better manage inbound and outbound product flow, thus providing companies with more visibility into their supply chains; and calculate rates and pricing. It's the job of Jordan Colletta, vice president of customer technology marketing, to add more customer value to UPS shipments. "We still move packages from A to B, the same as we did twenty years ago, but we've laid in value that reduces our customers' costs," Colletta says.

Then there are the six million daily receivers of UPS packages, a large portion of which are different every day. Perhaps someone interacts with UPS just three times a year when they order books from Amazon.com. UPS is committed to using technology to enhance their customer service and hopefully convince them to be more of an active, and not a reactive, customer.

For now, though, companies like Sears and YesAsia.com will remain UPS's focus, companies that use UPS technology to give their customers much more information about their products and shipments. As Daniel Swimm, co-founder of North Carolina candle supply company CandleScience.com, says, "Once the package is picked up, UPS is no longer a shipping company to me. It becomes my IT company."

That kind of customer intimacy is UPS's aspiration and what the one-to-one philosophy is all about. Eskew has at times voiced another take on one-to-one, a humorous wordplay on the phrase. If companies hire UPS to manage their entire supply chain, Eskew says, they will have "just one throat to choke." A joke, but a compelling argument: with today's enormously complex supply chains, global division of labor, and thousands of small players that don't provide anything close to a full complement of services, companies can choose one partner, governed by one vision, that can deliver one all-encompassing solution. Now that's a strategy for the future.

Speaking of the future, UPS will no doubt execute one of its trademark transformations in the years ahead in response to some yet unimagined challenge. How can one be so sure? As one former UPS executive says, "It's what we do."

The next chapter of the UPS story remains unwritten, but if the past holds any clues for what is to come, that transformation will result in not only a changed company, but a stronger company—one that will retain the best of what has worked in the past and adapt to meet a changing business world. That resilience is a testament to its homegrown leadership and ability to execute, certainly, but also to the singular culture planted by founder Jim Casey so long ago.

UPS RULES FOR THE ROAD

One Company, One-to-One

- **Take your vision global, quickly.** The interconnected global economy affords vast opportunities for companies to expand the markets for their products and services. UPS learned to develop solutions that anticipate customer needs and to provide them quicker than its competition.

- **Technology is the key to creating a one-to-one environment.** Customers demand focused attention on their business issues, and they want a one-stop solution. UPS learned how to use technology to serve its customers how they want to be served—to synchronize all the elements of commerce for a company—and treat them as if they are UPS's only customer.

Revealing the "Secret Sauce" at UPS

January 10, 2007

It's just a few days into UPS's centennial year. As your journey throughout UPS comes to a close, you can't help but reflect on an observation made by former UPS International chief Don Layden about the company's initial foray into West Germany in the 1970s: Once that package spigot is turned on, there's no turning it off.

With or without you—with or without any individual—the relentless pace of global commerce, of life at UPS, goes on. During the 2006 holiday season, UPS expected to hire 60,000 extra workers. On December 20, its peak day of the year, the company delivered more than twenty-one million packages, or about 240 every second. Every twenty-four hours, 1,800 UPS flights take off for more than 200 countries and territories.

With 2006 in the books, UPS has turned its attention to 2007 and all of its challenges: services to introduce (Delivery Intercept); hubs to build (Shanghai as a second major Asian hub); new routes to fly (augmented service to Bulgaria and Romania, admitted to the EU on January 1, 2007). In fact, somewhere, someone at UPS—in a conference room in Atlanta, a hub in Louisville, or on a computer terminal in Mahwah—is already deep in planning for next year's peak season, developing delivery schedules and modeling forecasts for potential package volume.

And you can picture, too, the UPSers you've met, and others like them, playing their own vital parts in the worldwide daily delivery drill that never stops. On a narrow cobblestone street in downtown Brussels, UPS Belgium driver Patrick De Keersmaecker explaining to an American art dealer how best to protect her paintings sent by UPS. Chicago-based Cindy Miller—the personification of the modern district manager at UPS—meeting with customers rather than running operations, the traditional role of the district manager. Gerhard Heinevetter, a German marketing manager, hurtling down the Autobahn to the Frankfurt ground hub to make sure things are proceeding without a hitch in the evening sort.

Other UPSers come to mind. Asia Pacific president Ken Torok wearing out his UPS policy book during regional meetings in Singapore. Jacek Przybylowski and Miroslaw Gral, two young managers at UPS Poland, signing up new dot.com customers that occupy Soviet-era buildings on the outskirts of Warsaw. In Shanghai, Supply Chain Solutions managing director Sebastian Chan figuring out ingenious ways for U.S. and European customers to cut steps out of their supply chain. And in Baltimore, Ranganath Nuggehalli and others from the Operations Research group, devising complex algorhythms to optimize the order in which drivers deliver packages.

And you wonder to yourself if you've really figured out how they collectively achieve this miracle of delivering fifteen million packages every day. Even with all of the Rules for the Road included in this book, you wonder if there isn't some other special approach, some defining trait, that allows UPS to be a trusted partner for customers ranging from German high-end fabric maker JAB Anstoetz, which makes curtains and upholstery for the world's finest hotels, to Patrick Enterprises of Circleville, Ohio, the world's largest manufacturer of monster trucks.

In the end, could it be as simple as one single secret? Actually, no. There is not one key ingredient to UPS's success, but three. And these three values certainly aren't secrets. In fact, they are well known to every company; it's just that some organizations don't have the leadership or capabilities to replicate them on a large scale. Above all, they are not complex management themes; UPS's success has never depended on theory or the "Eureka" moment.

That **culture** is the glue that holds the center at UPS will come as no surprise to anyone who has ever received a UPS package. But while customers view UPS's culture in terms of brown uniforms and resourceful drivers, UPS has actually used culture as a competitive advantage throughout its history.

For example, the culture of consistent promotion from within the company has forged the world's large corporate meritocracy and supplied UPS with far more bench strength than its competitors. Employees with talent are groomed for the next rung and often switch jobs every few years, and departments every five or ten. UPS managers are encouraged to train their replacements almost as soon as they begin a new assignment. Not only does this policy make for excellent training through-out the company, it gives employees the incentive to do their best, because they'll be noticed. UPS CIO Dave Barnes started working for the company as a part-time worker in St. Louis, un-loading packages on the sort, and he's not unusual in that he worked in operations, engineering, finance, and technology.

Not only is this corporate culture of nurturing talent unusual in corporate America, but it clashes with conventional manage-ment zeitgeist that companies should always search far and wide, often outside of the organization, for the "best and bright-est." UPS is doing something very different.

With this kind of attention focused on their careers, it's not surprising that the vast majority of full-time UPS employees have "skin in the game," another defining cultural trait. For ninety-three years out of its history, UPS was a privately owned com-pany, owned by its managers and former managers. This not only provided a dispersed group of managers throughout the country with common cause, but led them to make decisions based on the long-term health of the company, not on quarterly or annual revenue goals or some other short-term motive. As UPS would say, the company is managed for the next quarter-century, not the next quarter. Today, all employees are encour-aged to buy and hold the company's publicly traded stock.

It's okay to admit now. "Constructive dissatisfaction" has al-ways seemed to you like the name of an obscure theory of modern art or literature. But the point, you've come to see, is that while customers see the results of UPS's **ability to execute** on such a massive scale every day, they don't see what lies at the root of this constant tweaking. Former CEO Oz Nelson once put it this way to a reporter: "This is a business about pennies." A few pennies saved on millions of packages a day, then, can make all the difference.

For that reason, UPS measures every aspect of its operations, and has since early in its history, from how many left-hand turns a driver will encounter on a single route to the number of packages that it delivers each day worldwide.

One of the more compelling theories of execution at UPS is that it's management skill—not a specialized area of knowledge—that is the key to execution. Former chief information officer Frank Erbrick, for example, likely never troubleshot a single computer in his entire life before taking the CIO job, but he nonetheless helped execute one of the biggest technology transformations in modern corporate history. Chairman Mike Eskew is the former head of industrial engineering, and the CEOs immediately preceding him included two operators, a marketer, an attorney, and an accountant. As far as UPS is concerned, then, a good manager with broad experience trumps a subject matter expert.

Intensive training is also essential for UPS to execute at the high level that customers expect. UPS has Supervisory Leadership Schools and Management Leadership Schools for its future leaders, but employees at every level undergo extensive training. One of the benefits of so much training is that good decisions can be made at UPS on the spot by employees in the trenches. UPS executes locally, not from suburban corporate offices.

Drivers, for example, make hundreds of unsupervised decisions every day regarding how best to serve their customers.

A package-center manager in Turkey might decide to send a feeder truck straight to the airport instead of to the sorting center, and managers in Louisville sometimes decide on their own to charter a Lear jet to handle excess volume. The fact that UPS has just seventy expatriates out of 67,000 international employees underscores the power given to local managers, not just in the U.S., but worldwide.

With the ability to execute comes the vision to detect fool's gold. During the 1990s dot.com bubble, online business models were the craze. UPS even thought about throwing itself into the online grocery business before UPS engineers really dug into the market opportunity and concluded that it didn't offer enough scale and density to make a good business.

Perhaps the biggest surprise in the search for the "secret sauce" at UPS is the company's unlikely knack for **transformation,** particularly when most of us believe UPS has been doing essentially the same thing for a century. But look back to the mid-1980s, a point at which UPS was at the very top of its game. This is a company that could have shut the lights off, come back in 1990, and still have been in the black. Even given FedEx's success at next day delivery, for instance, UPS was still making approximately six times the profits on twice FedEx's revenue because of its ability to execute.

So what did UPS decide to do? Rip up the game plan and design a new business model, one that included serving Europe and Asia with a global delivery network. After the emergence of the Internet as UPS thrived as the delivery service of choice for e-commerce in the late-1990s, it again threw out the playbook and decided to embrace a new solutions-based strategy.

Even back in 1954, when the vast majority of UPS's revenues

still came from its lucrative relationships with thousands of well-known and respected department stores, Casey knew it was time to make the call: The company's future was in the common carrier business, not the retail business.

Simply put, transformation is in the company's DNA. And it keeps getting better at it.

Recently, for example, the company has expanded its capabilities by acquiring companies far smaller, nimbler, and more entrepreneurial than UPS. Initially, UPS was aggressive in transporting its culture into these new pieces of the company. It quickly learned, however, that the logistics business was less regimented and less predictable than the by-the-clock, standard delivery and pick-up-time world of UPS. As such, it gave subsequent acquisitions more latitude, which remains the case to this day.

So, pondering all this, you log onto the UPS Web site during the holiday season to get some packing tips. And there you find a piece of wisdom you won't find in any other management book: "Don't use old boxes when shipping; they lose their strength after being used and can subsequently collapse." There's pure UPS for you: simple, straightforward, but eminently practical and important advice. After all, nothing is more important to global commerce than a package—and a good strong box to send it in.